T0354394

GOING POSTAL,
THE STORY BEHIND
THE "FOREVER STAMP"

BY
ALLEN SANFORD

 www.trafford.com

North America & international
toll-free: 1 888 232 4444 (USA & Canada)
fax: 812 355 4082

ACKNOWLEDGMENTS

I would like to express my gratitude to the following people:

My Mother and Father

Congresswoman Barbara Lee

Associated Press Ralph Nader Christopher Shaw Shelly Dreifuss
Billy Copeland Don Teeter
Roberto Alcala

My fellow employees across the country especially those who worked on the bulk belt systems and at the container repair centers.

WHAT THIS BOOK IS ABOUT

THIS should be read as a compliant because that is what it is. This is a "Whistle-blower" complaint that is being reissued. This time it will be issued to the court of public opinion.

This complaint retraces the rise in postal rates and how those rate increases directly correlate with the acquisition of mail processing equipment. It will deal with the focus of the Postal Service, a focus that has shifted from delivery to processing because of the arrangements made with large corporations.

GOING POSTAL, THE STORY BEHIND THE "FOREVER STAMP"

O N October 10th, 2002 a postal employee was nearly electrocuted while working on mail processing equipment at the main post office in Oakland, California. This accident was covered up. The employee was intimidated into not filing an accident report. He was told that if he filed an accident report that he would face disciplinary action. As a witness I filed a "Safety Hazard Report".

In response to the "Safety Hazard Report", the manager stated that the accident occurred because of the inadvertent actions of the employee. This manager went on to say that the employee had been trained to do the job safely, but failed to do so. This was a lie.

The equipment that the employee was working on was not supposed to be in the building. The equipment was deemed obsolete in 1988. After the earthquake in the Bay Area in October of 1989, the Postal Service was instructed to remove all overhead conveyors and equipment. The instruction was ignored. The equipment remained and was allowed to deteriorate. When the employee was shocked; the equipment had deteriorated to the point that a screwdriver had to be used to activate the equipment from the panel box. 480 volts ran to these panel boxes. The system could not be shut down, the circuit was live.

This employee was not trained to work with electrical circuits. He was at the end of his postal career and was being forced to do this job under the threat of termination. After I filed the safety complaint he and the other lower level senior mechanics were required to take classes that were forbidden to them at the beginning of their careers.

What was being done to this employee was being done to employees in maintenance departments across the country. These people were in the old retirement system and the Postal Service wanted them out quickly. In this case, the equipment that was being worked on was being used to store third class mail. Mail would be allowed to sit in the bulk belt system for weeks at a time. This was being done by management because a place was needed to hide this mail until it was processed.

In response to the "Safety Hazard Report", the manager stated that the equipment had been maintained and that all of the mechanics assigned to work on the equipment had been trained. This was a lie. The mail that was being stored in the system was being used to pad the mail volume figures. The manager was submitting data as if the equipment was fully operational. This was a lie. Fraudulent data had been submitted since I participated in shutting down the equipment in 1989. The accident had to be covered up because the equipment was not supposed to be in the building. The bulk belt system in Oakland was the last to be taken out. Postmaster John Potter came to Oakland personally to get it done in 2006.

Fraud, favoritism, nepotism and outright corruption were the primary contributors to the hostile environment that existed in the Postal Service during the seventies and eighties. Add to this the poor response to grievances and E.E.O. complaints which could take years to resolve and you have a volatile mix that could and many times did cause violence. I stopped a number of fights and on occasion had to be restrained myself.

People brought weapons to work. Even the senior maintenance manager announced that he had a gun in the trunk of his car when he felt that he was being threatened by an employee. Actually the employee was stealing his girl friend who was actually married to someone else.

The assumption has been made on many occasions that Postal Workers are overpaid slackers who couldn't work anywhere else because postal skills are unique. There are some slackers everywhere.

In the Postal Service, the requirement that one had to adapt to new equipment every six months was daunting. New machines were being brought in during the seventies and eighties as fast as the postal service could buy them. When a new machine was introduced, personnel in the maintenance department would have to attend training sessions in Oklahoma.

A lot of people came to the post office right out of high school or out of the military in the early seventies when I was hired. The building had just been opened in 1968 and there were no computers. The mail was hand sorted in cases and the bulk belt system ran throughout the building. The place was filthy. You had to take a bath or a shower when you got home if you were a mechanic. We had to blow dirt and dust away each night before we could work on the equipment, and at times it would be an inch thick.

As new equipment was brought on line, things got more tense. Neither the managers nor the employees were computer literate. Some barely got out of high school. The Postal Service had to be dragged into the computer age. The transition was hard, and a lot of people got hurt and lost their jobs along the way.

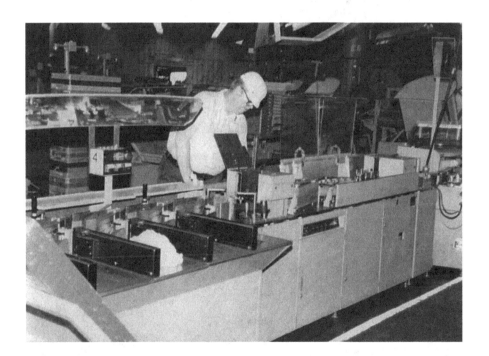

Mail processing equipment from the 70's&80's. Much more was purchased during the late 80's &90's and into 2000. You couldn't get your mail any faster unless you had Scotty beam it to you. Now there are no clerks on the floor. They are machine operators. The equipment *is scrapped before the end of it's useful life.*

To say that the environment was hostile would be an understatement. Add to it the drugs, sex and corruption, and you had to be ready for anything when you came to work. Managers and employees were operating by whatever rules applied to the section in which they worked. There was no uniformity regarding postal operations.

In 1997 Karla Corcoran was named as the first Inspector General for the newly created IG's office. Her first task was to stop the violence. She said, "From an IG's perspective we don't want to see employees retaliated against for reporting fraud, waste, abuse and mismanagement to offices like ours. Under the Inspector General Act there is a prohibition against retaliating against employees for bringing matters to the inspector general's attention". Ms. Corcoran went on to say, "The problem is there is no remedy in the Inspector General Act. So the Whistle-blower Protection Act would provide a remedy." Or at least that was what was supposed to happen. They tried to fire me many times and that is why you are reading this.

Please read these articles from the Associated Press. Notice how fast her departure came after her comments regarding contracting.

Government Executive Magazine ... ...

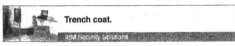

Trench coat.

HM Security Solutions

Free E-mail Newsletters | About Us | Contact Us | Index | Search | Advanced

Home	**E-mail**
Pay & Benefits	to a frie
Management	Printer
Homeland Security	version
Defense	See rea
E-Government	comme
Per Diems & Travel	your ow

Daily Briefing

May 2, 2003

Postal IG under fire for unusual 'team-building' activities

By Tanya N. Ballard
tballard@govexec.com

A government watchdog group and two senators have accused Postal Service Inspector General Karla Corcoran of wasting resources, and want her ousted from her position.

Corcoran "seems to have been too busy wasting her own agency's resources to have been much of a watchdog for the Postal Service," wrote Sens. Byron Dorgan, D-N.D., and Ron Wyden, D-Ore., in a May 1 letter to David Fineman, chairman of the Postal Service's Board of Governors.

The letter recounted whistleblower reports of IG employees building gingerbread houses, dressing up like 1970s-era disco group The Village People and performing striptease during work hours. The two lawmakers also criticized the amount of waste, fraud and abuse identified by Corcoran's office during her tenure in comparison with her expenditures.

"In 2001, with an IG staff of approximately 725 employees and an IG budget of $117 million, IG Corcoran identified only $56 million of waste at the Postal Service," wrote the senators.

A day earlier, Citizens Against Government Waste, a Washington-based interest group, forwarded a letter to Fineman asking that a new postal inspector

Dorg
letter

Relate
• Pos
may :
times
• Pos
reject
strike
for ul
(04/30
• Pos
paym
signe
(04/23
• Co
passe
redire
pensi
(04/0

January 28, 2002

 MONEYScope

Tip of the iceberg !!

FEATURED SERVICES
RELATIONSHIPS
SHOPPING
DOWNLOADS
WIRELESS

S&P PERSONAL
WEALTH

INTERACT
VIDEO & AUDIO
BOARDS
CHAT
NEWS ALERTS
CONTACT ABC

[x] Post Office

Questionable Bookkeeping?

Money-Losing Postal Service Used Accounting Trick to Pay Out Bonuses

By *John Martin*
abcNEWS.com

A U.S. Postal Police officer directs mail trucks from the parking lot of the West Trenton U.S. Postal Service Branch in Ewing, N.J., last October. (Daniel Hulshizer/AP Photo)

W A S H I N G T O N, Jan. 28 — Enron's troubles are not the same as the United States Postal Service's difficulties — not by a long shot. But newly released federal audits show the Postal Service also used questionable bookkeeping analysis to change the perception of its performance.

An insider's view on what makes the news...

MORE ON THIS STORY

> RELATED STORIES

• Some Say Post Office Has Few Options

• GMA: Stamp Prices Up Amid Postal Budget Bloat

• Post Office Weighs Letter Shortfall

Despite the efforts of more than 800,000 employees, the Postal Service is losing money. Yet audits by Inspector General Karla Corcoran show 80,000 postal managers received $805 million in bonuses while the service was losing $2 billion between 1998 and 2000.

It's called pay for performance, a way to make employees accountable. It worked fine in earlier years while the Postal Service was making a profit. But when it lost $2 billion between 1998 and 2000, officials found it hard to justify bonuses.

So postal executives decided to find a way. The method they chose was to artificially adjust the books for inflation, turning a billion-dollar loss into a $1.7 billion gain. They used a term pioneered in private business called "economic value added."

ALSO ON abcNEWS.com

• Mom Hopes Mystery Boy Is Her Son

• 'Silly Season' Begins in 2004 White House Race

• Lowly Fruit Fly's Amazing Flight Secrets

'Why Are You Paying Out Bonuses?'

The change was not reported on the books but was used to trigger the bonuses under the banner of pay for performance.

This raised a question by Inspector General Corcoran: "If you have no net income, why are you paying out bonuses?" She called the pay-out unreasonable.

"It's not reasonable because they're using an inflation adjustment factor ... and the CPI [consumer price index] to adjust what their revenue would be. There's really no justification for [this adjustment]."

THIS S
SMALL
MONE

SMALL B

AMERI
BUSIN
CLI

STOCK

00:09ET

10:00   noi
DJIA
NASDAQ

http://abcnews.go.com/sections/business/WorldNewsTonight/martin_usps_020128.html

5/7/2003

The Postal Service says it actually saved money this way because it no longer has to pay big cost of living raises or automatic pay raises, mechanisms relinquished some years ago in exchange for the bonus plan. Some managers complain that they are short-changed by the bonus plan.

Was Extra Pay Justified?

Was it justified in awarding the extra pay? Supporters point out that amounted to about $2,500 or less for each of the 80,000 supervisory or managerial personnel.

A spokeswoman affirmed the pay and the principle of bonuses while admitting that the service has lost money.

"When the economy suffers," says Judy de Torok, media manager, "the Postal Service suffers."

The Postal Service is suffering because it is run by crooks

Reminded that postal managers did not suffer because they still got bonuses even when business was down, de Torok insisted: "The financial performance of the institution is just one of several factors that go into the funding formula for pay for performance."

She cited faster mail delivery, better customer service, and greater workplace safety.

This is a lie !!

But Graef Crystal, a compensation analyst and columnist for Bloomberg News, calls the inflation-adjusted numbers "phony as a three-dollar bill."

Crystal, a veteran expert in the field of pay and benefits in New York and California, says the Postal Service should accept the reality of its financial condition.

Says Crystal: "A bonus plan, to my way of thinking, ought to operate on the principle that you live by the sword, you die by the sword." ∎

ATTENTION: BARGAINING UNIT EMPLOYEES

ACCORDING TO THE JULY 21, 1997 ISSUE OF THE FEDERAL TIMES, KARLA CORCORAN, THE NEW POSTAL SERVICE INSPECTOR GENERAL, WILL OPEN A TOLL-FREE INSPECTOR GENERAL HOTLINE ON AUGUST 4, 1997, FOR POSTAL EMPLOYEES WHO WANT TO REPORT FRAUD, WASTE, ABUSE, OR MISMANAGEMENT. THE NUMBER IS (888)USPS-OIG, (887-7644).

Fredric Jacobs, Executive Vice President

🖘 🖘 🖘 🖘 🖘 🖘 🖘 🖘 🖘 🖘 🖘 🖘 🖘 🖘 🖘

POSTAL SCENE

Inspector General Moving Ahead

By Chet Bridger
Federal Times Staff Writer

Six months after stepping into a newly created office, the new inspector general of the U.S. Postal Service is starting a hot line for reporting abuse, beefing up her staff and consolidating new powers.

Inspector General Karla Corcoran will open a toll-free inspector general hot line for postal employees August 4. Any employee who wants to report fraud, waste, abuse or mismanagement can call (888) USPS-OIG.

Corcoran said her primary interest is in "systemic" problems, but she wants to hear anything postal employees have to say.

"We want to hear from them, Corcoran said.

"We are trying to improve the system.

"If there are repeated personality conflicts, say with a particular manager, but the management on top of them never tend to deal with that at all, then we would certainly be interested in that," Corcoran said. "The only way you develop a trend is by hearing from these individual cases."

About 90 percent of initial complaints to Corcoran have concerned labor-management issues. Her office has heard from several employees involved in grievances and equal employment opportunity complaints, but the IG will hesitate to get involved with individual cases at early stages.

"Typically we're not going to get involved in those type of things until they've run through

whatever processes they have available to them. We're trying to look more at the systemic issues," Corcoran said. "But we respond to all of them no matter what."

The inspector general is independent of postal service management. Corcoran reports directly to the nine presidentially appointed members of the postal service Board of Governors and to Congress. She was appointed to a seven-year term by the governors and began in January.

Corcoran and her counsel want Congress to extend the Whistleblower Protection Act to postal employees.

"From an IG's perspective, we don't want to see employees retaliated against for reporting fraud, waste, abuse and management to offices like ours," said Thomas Coogan, counsel for the inspector general.

"Under the Inspector General Act there is a prohibition against retaliating against employees for bringing matters to the inspector general's attention. The problem is there is no remedy in the Inspector General Act. So the Whistleblower Protection Act would provide that remedy."

The new IG office is growing quickly. The staff grew from 36 on June 4 to 75 on July 10. Corcoran expects the staff to grow to 150 by September, and to as many as 500 in five years. Eighty-five positions in the IG office will be law enforcement jobs, complete with authority to carry weapons and make arrests.

The Postal Inspection Service has continued performing all audits and investigations. A memorandum of understanding allows Corcoran to take over inspector general functions from the inspection service as her office is staffed.

Coogan, formerly of the Federal Deposit Insurance Corporation, recently took over inspector general subpoena power from the inspection service.

Other authority soon will begin transferring between the two organizations.

Corcoran said two audit areas on her agenda are contracting and facilities.

"We're interested in looking at the contracting area because of the amount of contracting that are let by the postal service. We understand there's about $7 billion worth of contracting done out of the $55 billion budget. That's pretty good sized."

The inspector general will have an "East duty station" in the Washington, D.C., area and a "West duty station" in Dallas. Other field offices will be established in Minneapolis, St. Louis, and San Bruno, Calif.

New faces in the IG office include: Sylvia Owens, formerly with the Defense Criminal Investigative Service, now assistant inspector general for revenue and cost containment; Ronald Merryman, from the Air Force Audit Agency, assistant inspector general for employee and collection matters, from the Air Force Audit Agency, acting assistant inspector general for performance.

'I want to hear from [postal employees]. We are trying to improve the system.'

IG Karla Corcoran

washingtonpost.com

Postal Service IG Quits As Inquiry Concludes
Report Finds Pattern of Abuse and Waste

By Christopher Lee
Washington Post Staff Writer
Wednesday, August 20, 2003; Page A19

Karla W. Corcoran, the U.S. Postal Service inspector general, retired yesterday after a federal investigation found that she abused her authority, wasted public money and promoted questionable personnel practices.

The Postal Service's Board of Governors announced that David C. Williams, a former IG at four different agencies, would immediately take over as only the second inspector general in the history of the agency.

The investigation by the President's Council on Integrity and Efficiency found that Corcoran "followed a pattern and practice of unprofessional conduct in the management of the USPS OIG, used questionable judgment in areas within her discretion, extravagantly expended USPS funds, and engaged in personnel practices which were either questionable or not in accord with USPS policy," wrote Grant D. Ashley, chairman of the council's integrity committee.

The committee recommended that "the most severe administrative sanctions available be taken against Ms. Corcoran," Ashley wrote in a July 28 report cover letter to Clay Johnson III, council chairman and deputy director for management at the Office of Management and Budget. The council promotes professionalism among IGs and in U.S. agencies.

In a telephone interview yesterday, Corcoran used an expletive to characterize the findings of the council's 274-page report and said she had been made a scapegoat.

"They did not employ people that were familiar with postal operations," Corcoran said of investigators. "It's as much of an attack on the Postal Service itself as it is on me. They don't like a lot of postal practices, and so I became the catalyst."

Corcoran, who earned $142,500 a year, became the Postal Service's first IG after Congress created the office in 1996 to combat the perception that the chief postal inspector could not be objective. Corcoran's job was to root out waste and fraud at the Postal Service, which has 750,000 employees and a $65 billion budget. She said she identified $2.2 billion in potential and actual savings during her tenure. But critics, including a group of 55 current and former employees, complained of what they described as her overbearing, "values-oriented" management style, reckless spending and unfair personnel decisions.

Fear of retaliation and or termination is the reason why the employee who was shocked while working on the equipment, did not file an accident report. The employee was told by the manager that if he filed an accident report, he would face disciplinary action.

The following quote was taken from "Preserving the People's Post Office" by Christopher W. Shaw: "The Postal Service's activities in the parcel and express delivery markets are of concern to two of the most powerful corporations in Washington, D.C. - FedEx and UPS. They want to make sure that the Postal Service remains as ineffective a competitor as possible. And while they may be ideologically committed to the idea, as long as the Service keeps delivering packages, they will find privatization somewhat troubling, because it presents the possibility of giving the Postal Service greater freedom to challenge them competitively. Competitors and potential competitors in other areas are similarly concerned with hemming the Service in and containing it, so that it does not compete with them in any potentially profitable ventures. The corporate sector is also eager to see postal operations outsourced. Potential contractors and current competitors want the Postal Service to be privatized piece- by - piece, privatization in everything but name. In the interest of preserving universal service, the public should be wary of any attempts to slice off larger pieces of the postal monopoly, eliminate revenue sources such as package delivery, or disregard revenue sources in emerging markets related to postal services."

Mr. Shaw has done a very good job of analyzing the Postal Service from the outside. He has failed to consider the role that Postal Management has played in helping the process of privatization along.

Postal Management would like to privatize as long as their positions remain the same. The only people to suffer would be the employees. As it is, a number of Postal executives have defected to FedEx and to UPS. The manager in Oakland went to UPS after they came off a strike in 1997.

On January 29, 1993 I was given an award for special achievement. This award was given to me because I demonstrated to the people at the Container Repair unit how to repair General Purpose (GPC's) and Eastern Region(ERGPC's) mail containers.

The two award letters. On the award in 93 I suggested the computer kiosks be put into the lobby to give people information as well as stamps. The clerks didn't like it.

Special Achievement Award

is conferred upon

ALLEN SANFORD

in recognition of exceptional performance.

CONTAINER REPAIR CENTER

dated at

FRIDAY **AUGUST 29 1997**

**FOR YOUR
OUTSTANDING EQUIPMENT REPAIR EFFORTS
DURING THE 1997 UPS STRIKE
THE PACIFIC AREAS PERFORMANCE WAS
TOPS IN THE NATION**

UNITED STATES POSTAL SERVICE
CONTAINER REPAIR CENTER
OAKLAND CALIFORNIA

November 6, 1992

ALLEN   S
ALTHEA   K
BETTY   D
BILLY   C
CARL   R
CHARLES   L
DOUGLAS   F
EDDIE   H
EDDIE   S
FRANK   B
GEORGE   L
GILBERTO   R
HANEY   C
HUE   H
JAMES   M
JOHN   E
KENNETH   C
LAWRENCE   M
NOLAN G   D
PARLEE   R
PAUL   G
RD   M
RICARDO   B
SIDNEY   A
TIEN   A
VINCENT   M

Look at the award letter again. Befor I introduced new production techniques these people were scrapping equipment because they hadn't been shown how to repair it.

Multiply the number of people by the increase in production then by 28 locations across the country and you get some idea of how much was being scrapped.

We must put a stop in scrapping good, used wheels, and other capital equipment parts. As of today I'd like each one of you to save usable ones. I will take the time to scrutinize the scrap yard; we will not give away good government property.

Thank you.

Ramon S. Viray

cc: Joe Reel

"WE ARE WHAT WE DO"

Before I stepped in to instruct them in the repair of containers, these containers were being scrapped at a rate of 100 per day. Ten people were scrapping between $15,000 and $20,000 worth of equipment per day. This had gone on since the container repair center was opened 12yrs before I got there. In 1994, I filed a Whistle-blower complaint with the OIG's offices. I had sent a letter to Congresswoman Barbara Lee letting her know that the books were "cooked".

The numbers that I give you here are not speculative. They are the numbers that are reflected in the award letter and were calculated by the supervisor. There were 28 container repair centers across the country, and Oakland was the best in the Pacific Region. If we were the best and we were scrapping $20,000 worth of equipment per day what does that add up to on a nationwide basis.

Two employees were set up to take the fall for the theft of equipment from the Container Repair Center. The two employees were recovering Employee Assistance Program (EAP) participants, that is drug users. These two employees were assigned to the unit along with a couple of new employees one of whom was a postal inspector or agent. The supervisor who had given me the award had been removed and was replaced by a retired military man, an ex-Army staff sergeant. He was placed in the unit to facilitate the situation that would result in the two men being busted.

The letter of removal for one of the two employees who were set up to take the fall at the container repair center. After the letter is the petition that was submitted along with the grievance stating that the supervisor was allowing these people to leave while on t he clock. The supervisor got a promotion even though pornographic pictures taken by him were found in his desk.

UNITED STATES POST OFFICE

DATE: November 2, 1993

OUR REF: MHR:scs:94615-9405

SUBJECT: Letter of Decision - Removal

TO:

Sidney J Anderson   SS# 566-84-2392
Blacksmith Welder
Tour 2, P/L 787
Container Repair Center
Oakland CA 94615-2660

On September 27, 1993, you were issued a notice proposing to remove you, no earlier than October 30, 1993, from the U.S. Postal Service based on the charge outlined in this notice.

You did not answer the notice personally, nor did you provide any written information on your behalf. I find therefore, that the charge, as stated in the notice of September 27, 1993, is fully supported by the evidence and warrant your removal.

I have considered the fact that you violated the Standards of Ethical Conduct Regulations C.F.R.5: subpart A sections (a), (b) 5, 9, and 14 when you were charged with Unacceptable Conduct/Sale and Possession of a controlled substance on Postal Property. On September 15, 1993, in an interview with U.S. Postal Inspectors you admitted to five transactions of selling illegal narcotics. You admitted to using crack cocaine three times a week, the last time being three days earlier, <u>Although you did not admit to using crack cocaine at work.</u>

I have considered the fact that you violated the Employee Labor Relations Manual (ELM) Section 666.2 when you failed to conduct your self in a manner which reflects favorable upon the Postal Service by selling, and using illegal narcotics, <u>and by being intoxicated at work.</u>

the man was not !! busted.

I have considered that you violated the Employee Labor Relations Manual (ELM) Section 661.53 when your conduct at work was unacceptable in asmuch as you: <u>sold illegal narcotics to a co-worker.</u>

Only after this agent solicited the drugs and loaned the grievant money to take him, on the clock with the supervisor's knowledge, to get them.

Letter of Decision - Removal
Sidney J. Anderson
566-84-2392
Page 2

The Postal service was the one providing the scene of the crime and encouraging the crime.

I have considered that you violated the Employee Labor Relations Manual (ELM) Section 661.55 when you used Postal property for the illegal purpose of selling narcotics while on Postal property.
The Postal noticed a known EAP participant to backslide.
I have considered that you violated the Employee Labor Relations Manual (ELM) Section 661.53 when you chose to use illegal drugs when the ELM states, that the illegal use of drugs may be grounds for removal.

I have considered that you violated the Employee Labor Relations Manual (ELM) Section 661.86 and Section 666.3 when you failed to uphold the policies of the Postal Service by participating in illegal activities and repeatedly violating the ELM and the Standards of Ethical Conduct. The action will be effective November 5, 1993 *The postal service committed the unethical conduct of using the grievant as a scapegoat when the theft couldn't be found*
As a preference eligible, you have the right to appeal this decision in writing to Merit Systems Protection Board (MSPB), 525 Market Street, Room 240, San Francisco, CA 94105-2708, with in twenty (20) days from the effective date of this decision. If you appeal to the MSPB, you should state whether you or do not wish a hearing and you should furnish me a copy of your appeal. For further information on appeal procedures, contact Harvey Bell, Senior Labor Relations Specialist at (510) 874-8404. Attached for your reference are copies of the MSPB regulations and appeal form.

If you appeal this action, you will remain on the rolls but in a non-pay, non-duty status after the effective date of this action, until disposition of your case has been reached either by settlement or through exhaustion of your administrative remedies.

If you appeal to the MSPB you thereby waive access to any procedures under the National Agreement beyond Step 3 of the Grievance-Arbitration Procedures. You have the right to file as MSPB appeal and a grievance on the same matter. However, if the MSPB issues a decision on the merits of your appeal, if an MSPB hearing begins, if the MSPB closes the record after you request a decision without a hearing, or if you settle the MSPB appeal, you will be deemed to have waived access to arbitration. Further, if you have an arbitration, of if you appeal to the MSPB after the grievance has been appealed to arbitration, you will be deemed to have waived access to arbitration.

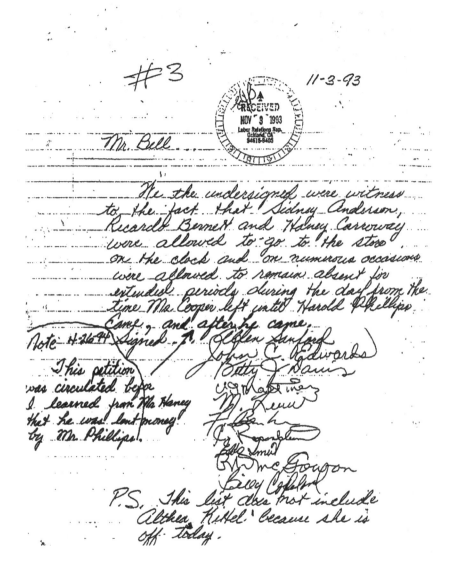

#3   11-3-93

RECEIVED
NOV 3 1993
Labor Relations Rep.
Oakland, CA
94615-8405

Mr. Bell

We the undersigned were witness to the fact that Sidney Anderson, Ricardo Bennett and Haney Carroway were allowed to go to the store on the clock and on numerous occasions were allowed to remain absent for extended periods during the day from the time Mr. Cooper left until Harold Phillips came, and after he came.

Note #26 Signed — *[signatures]*

This petition was circulated before I learned from Mr. Haney that he was lent money by Mr. Phillips.

P.S. This list does not include Althea Kittel because she is off today.

10/1/93

To Whom It May Concern...

During the arrest of Mr. Anderson and Mr. Burnet I was told by
one of the officers that an attempt was made to get a warrant
for my arrest but that there was not enough evidence.

Then I was advised by the officer to tell my fellow employees
that the stealing was going to stop. No mention was made of drugs.

Signed...

Frank Banks

CC..Harvey Bell,Labor Relations
John JeanPierre A.P.W.U.

*After Burnett and Anderson were busted 2048
Harold Phillips started bringing a camera to work.
Why did the inspector or agent leave?*

9

The agent was allowed to ride with these two people around town, looking for drugs. I filed a grievance which was ignored, and submitted with the grievance a petition signed by everyone in the unit stating that this was the fact. The two employees were busted anyway after a surprise (bogus) raid on the container repair center. During the bust, one other employee was detained but let go because he didn't fall for the trap. Not only was the new supervisor allowing these people to ride around town, he was getting paid by people in the unit if he would let them take off and would not put it in the attendance record.

This supervisor was also taking pornographic pictures of the neighborhood prostitutes with the camera that was provided to the unit to photograph safety hazards. Some of these photos would show this supervisor being serviced. This supervisor was not liked by the ladies in the unit. He made the mistake of leaving some photos in the desk drawer in the office. The secretary found them and the supervisor was removed from the unit. He got a promotion.

This is the type of equipment that was repaired or scrapped at the container repair center.

In August 1997, I was given another award for outstanding achievement. This time the award was for "Outstanding Equipment Repair Effort during the 1997 UPS Strike", (that is how it read). The award stated that the Pacific Area performance was tops in the nation.

Container repair in Oakland was closed at the end of 1999. There was no equipment left to be repaired. It had all been scrapped. Repair procedures that were issued in 1992 were never adopted on a nation wide basis. With minor repairs this equipment had a 10yr life span.

I wrote in a letter to the president of the Union that this was planned obsolescence and he agreed. Later that year he resigned from the Union and the Postal Service.

The way that this equipment was dealt with was the way that all postal equipment was dealt with in Oakland and I'm sure across the country as well.

When she took the position of IG in 1997 Karla Corcoran said "We're interested in looking at the contracting area because of the amount of contracts that are let by the postal service. We understand there's about $7 billion worth of contracting done out of the $56 billion budget. That's pretty good size."

I was told by a senior maintenance manager that the equipment at the container repair center was zero inventoried when it was purchased. I wondered
what he meant. It came together after I returned to the main office.

P&DC's (Processing and Distribution Centers)are like high volume factories
and run 24 hours a day, 7 days a week. They are staffed by a workforce made up
of full-time, part time, and casual employees whose weekly tours are subject to
labor laws, union contract, and local policies. At least they should be.

Marvin Runion dismantled the Labor Relations department when he became Postmaster. In doing this he ended the line of communication between
management and the employees. Then the Hatch Act Amendment of 93 took
the Congress and the Senate out of the picture.

The problem of scheduling the automated equipment in a P&DC with as
few workers as possible, required that management get around the union, the
Congress, and the Senate. Equipment was purchased at a break-neck speed
in the name of processing the mail. This equipment was dealt with the same
way that the equipment at the container repair center had been dealt with.
Equipment was and is never used to it's full life span and is needlessly modified
to annoy the employees more than anything else.

You don't get your mail any faster now than you did in 1990. The Postal Service
has acquired and scrapped millions of dollars of equipment in the name of mail
processing.

When Ms. Corcoran took over and looked at the books I am sure that she
was shocked. If she had been more patient she would have been able to witness
the mail disappear from the vans on the street and from the isles and elevators in
the large P&DC offices around the country. As the transition was made to the
bar-code and optical reader, the mail that was once hidden had now vanished
into the mail stream. Due to the bulk belt systems and the ability to hide and
store the mail, along with the dismantling of the Labor Relations Departments
and the institution of the Hatch Act Amendments, the mail volume numbers
were allowed to be inflated to the point at which they are today.

If the Postal Service was made to shift the focus of their business to delivery,
and required to get at least 80% of the useful life out of the equipment, that
would be a large savings. Real money could be saved however, by eliminating a
large segment of management, by contracting management out, and making the

employees the owners.

There are 80,000 managers in the Postal Service. A lot of these people are walking around doing nothing. The machines have eliminated the people. E.E.O. and EAP are both staffed by Postal employees. They are supposed to be neutral, but they aren't. Eliminate them.

The Union: The Clerks Craft and The Maintenance Craft don't like each other. The Clerk's Craft feels threatened by the Maintenance Craft. National grievances have been dealt with in arbitration when it comes to maintenance. The partnership between the Postal Service and the large companies who have a vested interest in processing the mail is too powerful.

The public has been shut out. Employee representation is nonexistent. Why not put the Postal Service on the stock exchange and let the employees own it. Contract out management and make delivery rather than processing the objective. Pre-paid mail is already sorted anyway, why does it need to be run through the machines.

The Union's Maintenance Craft is going to be without a seat when the music stops. The people who make the machines are going to require that only their personnel work on the equipment to ensure the warranty. Electronic technicians will become redundant; building maintenance will be next then the vehicle mechanics and the custodians. The clerks will be eliminated by the machines and the people who bring the mail to your house will be part time.

When Ms. Corcoran was made IG she knew that she would not have to deal with Labor Relations, safety or E.E.O. Had she not looked into procurement, she would still be the IG. Since her departure the issues that she raised have not been mentioned.

Ralph Nader, Shelley Dreifuss, and Christopher Shaw have skillfully explained how corporations are intent on highjacking the Post Office from the people.

This is being done in Europe. The Postal Service is being given until 2011 to sort things out. Privatization in Europe would be different because there are different countries.

The primary purpose of the Postal Service in America is to hold the country together and to ensure that the average American will not be discriminated against because of race, creed, economic or geographic region.

The Postal Service has been allowed to adopt its own accounting system. This system is based on how much mail is processed. 95% of the mail that is processed is processed by machines. According to the Postal Service's own sources, 23% of this mail is not delivered before the 10 day delivery cut off. Consider that a large portion of this mail is paid for in advance and is first class mail. The percentage goes up because this mail is pre-sorted and should not be run. Also there is mail that is processed even if there has been a change of address or the person is dead or the place is vacant. If delivery were tracked this would stop.

If delivery were the priority, the numbers would reflect the real number of people needed to move the mail.

Let the carriers be the owners of the Post Office. Contract management out.

Between 1998 and 2000 the Postal Service lost $2 billion. In 2001, IG Corcoran asked the managers, "If you have no net income, why are you paying out bonuses?"

After losing $2 billion the Postal Service changed accounting methods. They began to use a term called "economic value added". The change was not reported in the books but the new accounting procedure was used and the name was changed to "pay for performance."

When I returned to the main office, where there once were cases, there were now machines and a lot less people. The place was cleaner and the lighting had improved. Also, maintenance now had more control. Operations depended on the maintenance of the new machines. One machine can process more mail than was processed in the whole building at the time that I was hired.

I noticed something else after I lost my glasses while working on the bulk belt system. My glasses had dropped between the belts to the belts below me. All the belts were full from end to end with sacks. The belts would be surged to move mail through the system to slides where it would be taken to the machines for processing. The mail was not leaving the building. There was mail everywhere. The surge lines remained full at all times. There was mail in the elevators and isles. Mail was left in Vans in the yard and on the street for weeks at a time. Yet while all of this was going on, equipment was being purchased as if it was going out of style...and it was. It took me two weeks to get my glasses. The belts were not moved.

Equipment would become obsolete or need to be upgraded once and sometimes twice a year. Electronic technicians were made to go for training every year, sometimes two or three times a year to keep up. If they failed they were demoted. If they failed too often, they could be terminated. The lower level mechanics that had spent their entire careers at Container Repair Center were thrust into this atmosphere when they were returned to the main office. These people had been prevented from aspiring to become electronic technicians early in their careers. Now they were being forced under threat of termination to do the work without training. The equipment that they were forced to work on was life threatening. Due to the surge belts, the bulk belt system was always activated. This meant that every time a panel box was opened, you were exposing yourself to 480 volts of electricity. The employee was shocked because the handle used to turn the secondary current off was broken. Most of the handles in the system were broken. Screwdrivers were being used by the people who had been working on the equipment before we got there.

The man got shocked because this is how he was shown to do the job. Safety hazard reports had been filed. They were not being processed. When I filed a complaint with OSHA I was told that the issue would be looked into and Management was instructed to correct the situation. Two days after the instruction was given the employee was shocked.

Look at the date on the Safety Hazard Report. It was written 7 months after the grievance response to the man getting shocked on 10/12/02. OSHA was contacted on 10/02/02 The equipment was not suppose to be in the building. The grievance response is numbered. My hand written response has corresponding numbers.

REPORT OF HAZARD, UNSAFE CONDITION OR PRACTICE   [Assigned by safety office] 0 3 7 9 4

I. Employee's Action · X

Area (Specify Work Location) *Oakland Main Office Box 42*

De Hazard, Unsafe Condition or Practice. Recommended Corrective Action

The discription of the hazard, unsafe condition, practice and the recomended corrective action, is explained on the following pages. This is page 1 of 5.

Management has 48 his to respond. A control # is expected.

1.

Employee Received
2013
Oakland
94615-9997

Signature *Allen J. Sanford*   Date and Tour 7/14/03 Tour II

II. Supervisor's Action

Recommend or Describe Specific Action Taken to Eliminate the Hazard, Unsafe Condition or Practice. (If Corrective Action Has Been Taken, Indicate the Date of Abatement.)

There is no hazard, unsafe condition or practice as outlined in this PS form 1767. Employees assigned to work the bulk belts have had OJI training, lock-out tag-out training. All maintenance mechanics who have not completed basic electricity are required to complete the course.

Supervisor   Signature [illegible]   Date 7/14/03

III. Approving Official's Action
(Check One and Complete)

The Following Corrective Action was Taken to Eliminate the Hazard, Unsafe Condition or Practice (Indicate Date of Abatement):

A Work Order Has Been Submitted to the Manager, Plant Maintenance, to Effect the Following Change:

X There Are No Reasonable Grounds to Determine Such a Hazard Exists. This Decision Is Based Upon:

SEE ATTACHED STEP 2 Grievance # MA-73a-02, FWT/IF-G-022 4/46. All employees are encouraged to report HAZARDS & Accidents. There has Not Been retaliation on an employee for reporting hazards or unsafe conditions. Any unsafe condition is corrected as soon as possible. Employees are not working unsafely on the Bulk Belt System. Employees are being given training as required.

Approving Official   Signature [illegible] 7/L   Date 7/14/03   Date Employee Notified 7/14/03

IV. Maintenance Action (Complete If Necessary)

Maintenance Supervisor   Signature   Date   Date Hazard Abated

PS Form 1767, Dec. 1982   WHITE—Local Safety Office (After Abatement)   PINK—Local Safety Office (Initial Notice)
YELLOW—Approving Official   BLUE—Employee

Allen Sanford   GOING POSTAL

UNITED STATES
POSTAL SERVICE

January 26, 2003   Certified No. 7002 2410 0002 9247 3654
                                                  Return Receipt Requested

STEP 2 GRIEVANCE DECISION -   Installation: Oakland P&DC
                       •   Installation Finance # 05-5509
                              Grievant's Name: Allen Sanford
                              Grievant's SSN: 555-76-2114
                              Incident Date:
                              Local Union #: MA-732-02
                              Local Maintenance Management #:
                              Labor Relation #: F00T-1F-C-02246467

MICHAEL L. HINES
AMERICAN POSTAL WORKERS UNION
7700 EDGEWATER DRIVE SUITE 656
OAKLAND CA 94621-3022

Receipt is acknowledged of a step 2-grievance form, which alleges management, is in violation of Article 14 of the National Agreement. As a result, a step 2 discussion was held between you and me on January 7, 2003. Time frames to meet were extended by mutual agreement. All relevant facts were discussed and understood.

The Union contends that Management is in violation of the above noted article of the National Agreement by jeopardizing the health, safety and postal career of Grievant, Allen Sanford due to union activity and incompetence.

The requested remedy by the Union is that Grievant, Allen Sanford or Supervisor, Maintenance Operations, Anthony Butler be removed from crew 32 immediately and that the Grievant be compensated penalty pay retroactive to 9/6/02 for all hours the Grievant has to continue to be in crew 32.

After careful review of the relevant facts and documents in this case and based on the particular circumstances, **this grievance is denied.** The reasons for my decision are as follows:

The allegations made in this Grievance are the same as the allegations made in Grievance MA-646-02, Labor Relation# F00C-1F-C03032469. The issues brought up are the same, which were addressed in that Grievance. It appears that the Grievant did not agree with the step 2 decision in MA-646-02 and has filed another Step 2 dealing with the same issue. The Grievant is not being retaliated against by Management for any EEO or Union activity that he is involved. The Union has not presented any evidence to support a claim of retaliation. The Union is also unaware that an accident report has been completed for an accident involving Billy Copeland who incorrectly tried to restart a bulk belt conveyor. This accident did not result in an injury that required first aid or any other medical treatment. The Union has not presented any evidence to support its claim that Management is trying to save money to the detriment of safety for employees.

1615 7TH STREET
OAKLAND, CA 94615
(510) 874-8315
FAX. (510) 433-7537

STEP 2 GRIEVANCE DECISION
Local Union #: MA-732-02
Labor Relation #: F00T-1F-C-02246467
Page 2

What follows is a recap of the response in Grievance MA-646-02 that addresses the same issues raised in this Grievance. This response shows that Management is interested in the health and safety of employees working in the Maintenance Unit and has taken steps to correct safety related problems as they are found.

The Union claims that Management has allowed Maintenance Mechanics, PS-04 and PS-05 to work unsafely on the Bulk Belt System. This is not true. All Maintenance Mechanics, PS-05 performing work on the bulk belt system have been trained in Lockout/tagout procedures (see attached Individual Training Records for 4 mechanics). Employees have been trained to use lock out procedures if work needs to be done on a conveyor belt and the employee could be harmed if the machine were to start. There have been several On-the-Job Safety Review/Analysis (JSA) developed during calendar year 2002 for the bulk belt system to prevent accidents and keep employees working safely on the bulk belts (see 4 attached On-the-Job Safety Review/Analysis forms). #2

There is a sign posted on the motor control panels that warn all what not to do on the bulk belts (see attached picture of motor control panel). This sign states "Caution – Maintenance Personnel Only – 480 volts inside panel – do not push motor starter with bare hand or other device – keep panel door locked at all times. The JSA for Jogging conveyors and deflectors or manually positioning machinery or bulk conveyors is also attached to each motor control panel (see attached picture of motor control panel). #3

Any time that the Supervisor becomes aware that employees are performing a task unsafely, this is addressed and the employee is shown the safe and correct way to perform the task. This is what occurred with Maintenance Mechanic, PS-05, Billy Copeland. Once Supervisor, Maintenance Operations, Anthony Butler became aware of how Mr. Copeland had tried to restart a bulk belt conveyor, he immediately told the employee to stop. He also told all others the proper way to restart the belts. These mechanics do not work on motor starters. They are not required to work on motor starters. When they have a problem that requires additional troubleshooting beyond what they can do, Maintenance Mechanics PS-05 have been instructed to obtain assistance by notifying the Supervisor. #4 #5

The Union requests that Maintenance Mechanics, PS-04 and PS-05 who have worked on box 42 and motor starters be paid retroactively at the PS-07 rate. Management does not agree with this request. The bulk belt system runs on Tour 2 and Tour 3. These are the tours where box 42 operational maintenance takes place. These two (2) tours do not have Maintenance Mechanics, PS-04 on the rolls. There are only two (2) Maintenance Mechanics, PS-04 employees in LDC 36. Both of these employees are on Tour 1. Management therefore does not assign box 42 work to PS-04 mechanics. Management does assign Maintenance Mechanics, PS-05 to box 42 tasks. The majority of the work performed on the bulk belt systems (box 42) by Maintenance Mechanics, PS-05 involves removing sacks that are blocking photocells, clearing sacks off of slides, pulling sacks off of belts that are not running (dead belt), or pushing reset buttons on the motor control panel to restart a belt that has stopped running for a variety of reasons. Tour 3 does not have Maintenance Mechanics, PS-05 performing box 42 work. Tour 3 does not have authorized positions for Maintenance Mechanics, PS-05. Maintenance Mechanics, PS-05 who perform this task on Tour 2 are; A. Sanford, B. Copeland, and R. Salditos. #6

Allen Sanford GOING POSTAL

STEP 2 GRIEVANCE DECISION
Local Union #: MA-732-02
Labor Relation #: F00T-1F-C-02246467
Page 3

Attached are eighteen (18) Bulk Belt Conveyor and SSM Trouble log sheets completed by these mechanics during the month of October, 2002 that further verifies the type of work being performed by PS-05 mechanics. This is not the type of work that requires the skills of a Maintenance Mechanic, PS-07. The work that is performed by these mechanics is well within the duties and responsibilities of Maintenance Mechanics, PS-05.

The qualification standard (see attached bargaining unit qualification standard 4749) for 4749 Maintenance Mechanic, PS-05 states that it is a requirement for these mechanics to have 1) Knowledge of basic mechanics refers to the theory of operation, terminology, usage, and characteristics of basic mechanical principles as they apply to such things as gears, pulleys, cams, pawls, power transmissions, linkages, fasteners, chains, sprockets, and belts; and including hoisting, rigging, roping, pneumatic, and hydraulic devices. 2) Knowledge of basic electricity refers to the theory, terminology, usage, and characteristics of basic electrical principles such as Ohm's Law, Kirchoff's Law, and magnetism, as they apply to such things as AC-DC circuitry and hardware, relays, switches, and circuit breakers.

The Union claims that the preventive maintenance on the bulk belt system has been neglected. This is not true. Attached is the PM Activity By Acronym Report which clearly shows that the bulk belt system is being maintained. Preventive Maintenance on the bulk belt conveyors is performed by mechanics on Tour 1.

The Union claims that Maintenance Mechanic, PS-05, Allen Sanford, is being forced to take a course in industrial electrical services (IES) because of an inadequate staffing package which requires lower level employees to do higher level work of a Maintenance Mechanic, PS-07 without being paid. This is not true. As you can see from the qualification standard for Maintenance Mechanic, PS-05, knowledge of basic electricity is a requirement for the position. Allen Sanford has not completed the course for Basic Electricity. He is now enrolled in this course so that he can perform work that is expected of a Maintenance Mechanic, PS-05. This has nothing to do with the staffing package, but rather fitting the task to be performed with the position that can perform the task. Maintenance Mechanics, PS-05 are not expected or required to work with 480-volt electrical circuits. However, they should know basic electricity as required to perform their jobs in a safe manner. This is the reason all Maintenance Mechanics, PS-05 are required to complete the Basic Electricity Course.

The Union also claims that Management is covering up the fact that they have an inadequate staffing package to provide a safe working environment for the maintenance craft on all 3 tours by utilizing untrained lower level mechanics to perform higher level work because of budget restraints. This is not true. If anything, Management is more heavily weighted with higher level positions that what is required or actually needed (see attached FY 2003 Staffing Authorization). In LDC 36, where box 42 work takes place, Maintenance Mechanics, PS-05 and PS-04 make up only 10.1% of the work force. Clearly, a budgetary issue is not the case. Management is working to become more balanced in lower level positions. A more balanced work force would show approximately 20% of Maintenance Mechanics, PS-05 to total authorized staffing in LDC 36. The workload is there to support this mix.

29

STEP 2 GRIEVANCE DECISION
Local Union #: MA-732-02
Labor Relation #: F00T-1F-C-02246467
Page 4

The Union has not shown that Management has violated Article 14 of the National Agreement. The Union has not presented, nor can I find any evidence that Management violated any articles of the National Agreement in this case.

Therefore, for the above stated reasons, the grievance is denied.

PORTIA MUNN
MANAGER, MAINTENANCE OPERATIONS - TOUR II
OAKLAND P&DC

Attachments (7)

cc: MM
    Labor Relations (File Copy)

#1. The Union is unaware that an accident report had been made because none had been made. Mr. Copeland wasn't aware of it either.

There are numerous pannel boxes that must be opened to re-start the belts because of no preventative maintenance.

First a secret accident report is made then Mr. Munn makes the medical determination that no medical treatment was required. Did she check to see if he had an irregular heartbeat?

#2. While performing box 42 duties Lockout/tagout procedures are not used. The objective is to keep the system running. The routsheet requires that any breakdown over 15 min. is to be reported to the supervisor.

Surge-lines are not locked out while jams are removed. If the surgelines were locked out the jam could not be moved.

#3. The signs were not posted on the motor control panels until I filed a grievance with OSHA.

#4. The only way Mr. Copeland could have performed this task was the way he did it.
Don Teeter, electronic technician, was on box 42 the day Mr. Copeland was shocked. He should be enterviewed.

#5. The reset buttons on the outside of the boxes don't work in most cases and notifying a supervisor everytime a belt needs to be restarted is not done.

#6. Mr. Archibald has been assigned box 42, he is a custodian on detail. A review of logsheets would show that box 42 is much more than what is stated here. Again consult Don Teeter

#7. This PM Activity Report is fraudulant. I dropped my glasses on X-surge and could not get them for two weeks.
Go back to the night Peter Allen

discovered the 70 vans of mail in the yard. Check the breakdown reports against the mail volume numbers for the sack sorter on all tours at that time.

#8&9. Maintenance Mechanics B-05 have been required work with 480-volt "live" circuits for as long as there has been a box 42.

#10. As Maintenance Craft Director I informed then manager Joe Reel that he was making a mistake by hiring so many ET's off the street. He should have brought them in as level 6 MPE and worked them up.

#11. If the workload is there to support a 20% mix and there is only 10% here then why are level 5's being required to do higher level work and why can't more custodians get detailed to level 5?

This is contenuing "Waste Fraud & Mismanagement.

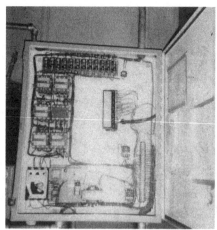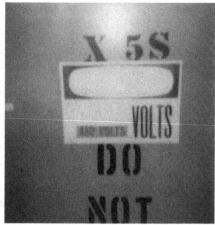

After closing container repair some of the people were expected to work on panel boxex that had live circuits(480 volts) even when the door was open.

"The Union is also unaware that an accident report has been completed for an accident involving(name excluded) who incorrectly tried to restart a bulk belt conveyor. This accident did not result in an injury that required first aid or any other medical treatment. The Union has not presented any evidence to support its claim that Management is trying to save money to the detriment of safety for employees." This was the statement made in response to my grievance by the senior maintenance manager. Secret accident reports were being kept and not sent to the safety office. The man who was shocked was never told that a report had been filed.

The equipment that the man was working on should not have been in the building. It should have been removed after the earthquake. Since the earthquake, the equipment was being used to store the mail. The manager was turning in figures as if the equipment was working normally, and the mail was being processed normally.

The mail was being run through the system as many times as was needed to make the mail volume figures acceptable. When this was done and the mail on the belts got low more would be brought in from the vans in the yard and the process would begin again.

Machines were being purchased but third class mail was not being delivered. Why?

On March, 9 2004 Shelley Dreifus made this statement to the Senate

Committee on Government Affairs concerning Postal Reform: Sustaining the 9 million Jobs in the $900 Billion Mailing Industry (Day 1). "The Postal Service has elected not to collect information on much of the bulk business mail that it handles, including bulk First Class and Standard Mail, and Periodicals. I am the recipient of weekly e-mailed reports of a planet-code tracking company called Mail Trak. Mail Trak collects the tracking information made available from Postal Service bar-code readers at Processing and Distribution Centers facilities through a new service called Confirm that the Postal Service offers. Purchasers of Confirm service, generally bulk First-Class Mailers and Standard Mailer, use Mail Trak company to collect tracking information and relay it to them in a user-friendly form. Mail Trak aggregates performance information from its customers and distributes the aggregate results in a weekly newsletter. In the past year, Mail Trak reports that approximately 23% of Standard Mail letters were being delivered later than the service standard window of 7-10 days. This valuable information that Mail Trak is able to provide only for its customers mailings. The Postal Service, on the other hand, could collect and report tracking information for all postal Confirm customers. The Postal Regulatory Board should be given the power to define the essential elements (or service standards) for each special service ancillary to non-competitive products, to require measurement of the performance of the service standard, require measurement of the performance of the service standard, require submission of the data collected, and to disseminate the performance results to the public."

GOING POSTAL   *Allen Sanford*

The statement made to the Committee on Homeland Security and Government Affairs by
Shelly Driefuss.

WITNESS TESTIMONY

Statement of Shelley Dreifuss
Senate Committee on Governmental Affairs
"Postal Reform: Sustaining the 9 Million Jobs in the $900 Billion Mailing Industry
(Day 1)"
March, 09 2004

Thank you for the opportunity to testify before this distinguished Committee on
Governmental Affairs regarding the recommendations of the President's Commission on
the U.S. Postal Service. It is an honor and privilege to share my views with you.

Postal reform is a matter of great importance to our economy, and of vital interest to the
users of postal services. This includes, of course, the many large mailers and their
associations and representatives who have and will continue to regularly present their
views to you; but users of postal services also include the hundreds of millions of
consumer and small business mailers who depend on regular mail delivery to their
residences and places of businesses. In addition, consumer and small business mailers
rely on easy access to the purchase of vital postal services through retail facilities and
other means. Above all else, they seek affordable and high quality postal services.

Role of the Consumer Advocate Currently and Under Postal Reform

As Director of the Office of the Consumer Advocate at the Postal Rate Commission, I am
charged with representing the interests of senders and recipients of mail who otherwise
would not be represented in Commission rate, classification, and complaint proceedings.
While individuals and small businesses generate or receive nearly 80% of postal volume
(approximately 160 billion pieces of mail in 2002), their individual expenditures for
postage and other services – on the order of $7/month – are likely to be too small a
percentage of their household and business budgets either to cause them to participate
individually in Postal Regulatory Board proceedings, or, alternatively, to associate as a
group to represent their interests. This has certainly been the case in the three and a half
decades since the Postal Reorganization Act was passed by Congress. There is every
reason to believe that this condition will persist after postal legislative reform.

In enacting the Postal Reorganization Act of 1970, your predecessors had the foresight to
assure participation by an "officer of the Commission who shall be required to represent
the interests of the general public." The requirement for such participation eventually led
the Commission to establish an office – the Office of the Consumer Advocate – to always
be on the ready to protect individuals and small businesses in the conduct of regularly
filed major and minor classification cases and periodically filed omnibus rate cases and
complaint cases set for hearings.

On July 12, 1999, the Commission adopted a Mission Statement that clarified the role of
the Office of the Consumer Advocate. According to the terms of that Statement, my office
has the following responsibilities:

· Be a vigorous, responsive, effective advocate for reasonable and equitable treatment for
the general public in Postal Rate Commission proceedings

· Give a strong voice to consumers, especially those whose interests are not otherwise
represented in Commission proceedings

· Present evidence and arguments on behalf of consumers in Commission proceedings

· Promote fair competition between the Postal Service and its competitors for the ultimate
benefit of consumers

I must emphasize that the Office of the Consumer Advocate at the Postal Rate
Commission is the only entity in the nation that represents the distinct interests of
consumers and small businesses before the Postal Rate Commission. In numerous
proceedings before the Postal Rate Commission, the Office of the Consumer Advocate has
litigated on behalf of low-volume mailers to ensure their access to benefits proposed only
for high-volume mailers. I will describe two examples. In 1999, the Postal Service
requested that the Postal Rate Commission issue a recommended decision for a new, low-
cost Bulk Parcel Return Service. The Postal Service proposed a mailer threshold of 50,000
pieces annually. Before entering into a settlement with the Postal Service to conclude the
proceeding without hearings, the Office of the Consumer Advocate convinced the Postal
Service to allow mailers that were one-fifth the size of those originally targeted by the
Postal Service to participate, thereby securing access to the service by the small business
community.

Recently, in the Negotiated Service Agreement ("NSA") case that the Postal Service and
Capital One brought before the Postal Rate Commission, at the insistence of the Office of
the Consumer Advocate, the Postal Service agreed to establish a formal process allowing
First-Class Mailers smaller than Capital One to negotiate NSAs along the same lines as the
Capital One agreement. Without Consumer Advocate representation of small mailer
interests, it is doubtful that this process would have been put in place.

The President's Commission Report contains no explicit recommendation for a statutorily
required consumer/small business representative, with funds for representation provided
by postal revenues. However, the current Postal Reorganization Act does so provide, and
it is my position that the Office of the Consumer Advocate (or a similar office) should be
designated explicitly in postal reform legislation. I should add that the Postal Rate
Commission addressed the need for consumer representation in Comments submitted to
this distinguished Committee on November 19, 2003. The Commission stated that there
might be sound policy reasons for ensuring a meaningful role for "captive customers,"
especially in those instances when the Postal Service might seek increases in captive
customer rates above the rate of an inflation-based cap. As explained earlier, meaningful
participation on behalf of captive customers will only be possible with a statutorily
designated, postal funded consumer advocate. Of course, the role of the consumer
advocate in the postal reform environment should parallel the role of the Postal
Regulatory Board. In the new era, the consumer advocate should represent captive
mailer interests in proceedings to increase their rates; proceedings to change or add new
mail classifications; and proceedings to define postal service standards and level of
performance. In addition, the consumer advocate should be given the power to file
complaints about unauthorized rate increases; cross-subsidization by them of other non-
captive classes of mail; and possible degradation in the quality of postal services.

The Postal Service's Mission: to Fulfill Consumer and Small Business
(as Well as Large Business) Needs for Postal Services

The President's Commission recognized the importance of the Postal Service to consumers
and small businesses. In Recommendation B-2, the President's Commission
recommended that the mission of the Postal Service be "to provide high-quality, essential
postal services to all persons and communities by the most cost-effective and efficient
means possible at affordable and, where appropriate, uniform rates." This is an excellent
summary of what the Postal Service means to consumer and small business users of the

Postal Service.

Traditional, Core Postal Services. The first distinct element of the President's Commission recommendation is to limit the activities of the Postal Service to core, traditional activities. These are the accepting, collecting, sorting, transporting, and delivering of letters, newspapers, magazines, advertising mail, and parcels. I am in full agreement with this limitation.

At the time of Postal Reorganization in 1970, Congress was comfortable in delegating its constitutional power to provide postal services to the nation in a form, and within the limits, known to it at that time. The Postal Service had not yet embarked on a course of competition with providers of electronic communication services in the private sector. Examples of partially electronic services that the Postal Service now claims are outside the jurisdiction of the Postal Rate Commission or any agency are ebill-Pay, a bill-paying service that members of the public may use to have their bills paid electronically or by mailed checks, and Netpost Card Store, a service available through the Postal Service's website that consists of greeting card purchases made by typing in the message for the card, paying by credit card, and eventually having a private company print and mail the greeting card for processing, transportation, and delivery by the U.S. Postal Service. Both of these products are in direct competition with private sector services.

GAO reports issued in the last five years indicate that the Postal Service is not an effective competitor in areas outside its traditional expertise. As a representative of consumer interests, I do not see any benefit in having the Postal Service compete with efficient, innovative entrepreneurs in the private sector. The harm done to consumers when the Postal Service ventures into new, unfamiliar commercial activities is to force captive consumers to fund money-losing experiments that discourage efficient, innovative private companies from offering comparable services. In the absence of the distortions in the marketplace produced by a government monopolist cross-subsidizing experimental commercial ventures, the forces of competition should work to produce high quality, inexpensive, innovative products that may be purchased by individual consumers and small businesses.

The clearest evidence of my commitment to this view is the role my office played to support the efforts of a San Francisco-based organization, Consumer Action, to petition the Postal Rate Commission to clarify its jurisdiction over non-traditional services and, at the least, to establish detailed accounting and reporting rules for any non-traditional commercial activities (such as all-electronic communications products) that the Postal Service claims are not subject to the authority of the Postal Rate Commission. In response to the Consumer Action petition, the Postal Rate Commission commenced two new rulemaking proceedings: the first proposes a definition of services subject to Postal Rate Commission jurisdiction; and the second proposes the institution of new accounting and reporting requirements for non-jurisdictional products and services.

In comments on the Postal Rate Commission's proposed rulemaking to define postal services, the Association for Postal Commerce ("PostCom") wrote that the addition of the word "physical," as in physical delivery, acceptance, collection, sortation, and transportation of mail would make it very plain that the Postal Service has not been given license to engage in electronic communication services. I agree that the addition of the word "physical" would be a crucial addition because it would keep the Postal Service out of marginally related and non-related commercial activities.

In the November 19 Comments submitted to this Committee by the Postal Rate Commission, the Commission stated that clarifying national policy on appropriate areas of Postal Service business would answer vexing policy questions and reduce (or eliminate) contentious Postal Rate Commission proceedings on the Postal Service's authority to enter into non-traditional commercial areas. I fully agree with the Postal Rate Commission that clear guidelines in postal reform legislation would resolve this unsettled legal question.

Just two weeks ago, a complaint was filed with the Postal Rate Commission by a small business called DigiStamp. DigiStamp has been an early provider of electronic time/date stamps for electronic files. DigiStamp is very concerned about a nearly identical, new, U.S. Postal Service product called Electronic Postmark. DigiStamp voiced understandable concerns that a $70 billion enterprise, with captive customer revenues, can compete unfairly with DigiStamp. The Postal Service claims that Electronic Postmark is outside the Commission's jurisdiction and has resisted attempts to make a full accounting for the costs of developing and operating this service. If the Postal Service is cross-subsidizing Electronic Postmark with captive customer revenues, a small startup company like DigiStamp may easily be driven out of business unfairly; and captive customers will sustain a double injury: they may be cross-subsidizing Electronic Postmark to their disadvantage as mailers, and they may be deprived of innovative, high quality, low cost private sector services that cannot compete with a $70 billion monopoly-funded enterprise.

I agree with the President's Commission that the Postal Service should not be permitted to continue such non-traditional competitive forays in the future. The President's Commission's recommendation for resolution of the question, i.e., to limit the Postal Service to its traditional postal activities, is the best way to prevent such conflict in the future.

The President's Commission also recommends a Postal Regulatory Board complaint mechanism that would allow members of the public to file complaints with the Postal Regulatory Board on the ground that the Postal Service is engaging in activities that fall outside its core mission. In my opinion, a statutorily designated consumer representative should be among those who may file such a complaint.

Universal Service. While I would limit the Postal Service to traditional postal activities, I believe that the interests of consumers, particularly those living in non-urban regions of the United States, are best served if the Postal Service is obliged to provide delivery services and to continue to offer the sale at retail of letter, package, and ancillary special services. Rural consumers may not have ready access to the private delivery services that are more plentiful in densely populated areas. Even urban consumers may be unable to gain ready access to private delivery services. For this reason, it is important to preserve consumer and small business access to postal letter, package, and ancillary special services.

Consumers, small and large businesses, and federal, state, and local governments all need regular, timely delivery to their home and business addresses. In view of the great need for retail and delivery services across the nation, I support the President's Commission recommendation that the Postal Service continue to be charged with a universal service obligation.

Governmental Services. The second element of the President's Commission recommendation on an appropriate mission for the Postal Service is to allow the Postal Service to engage in one additional set of limited activities: providing other governmental services when in the public interest and where the Postal Service is able to recover the appropriately allocated costs of providing such services. At the time of Postal Reorganization, Congress regularly enlisted the aid of the Post Office to furnish services to the public through postal retail facilities. The Post Office was uniquely positioned to provide such assistance. A postal historian from Oxford University, Gerald Cullinan, explains the reason for giving the Post Office (later the Postal Service) this role. In the "Nonpostal Functions" section of his historical account,1 Cullinan states that "because of its ubiquity in American life" the Post Office "was called upon to perform a bewildering number of nonpostal functions pro bono publico." Also, Mr. Cullinan explains, "there has been a steady accretion of minor federal functions . . . mainly because, in many communities, the post office is the only federal office in town and the center of local activities." These included the sale of Liberty bonds and war savings certificates; registration of aliens; sale of U.S. savings bonds; sale of documentary stamps; notary public services; and accepting passport applications.

I concur with the President's Commission's formulation of a suitable role for the Postal Service in providing governmental services to the public on behalf of other governmental agencies, and commend the President's Commission for couching this role in terms of governmental services. The use of "nonpostal" in the Postal Reorganization Act has produced widespread confusion and contention in the postal community, particularly since the Postal Service has used the term in a manner the legislative history indicates was never contemplated by your predecessors in 1970, i.e., to engage in a wide range of nonmail, non-traditional, nongovernmental activities that are in competition with the private sector.

The Scope of the Postal Monopoly

The President's Commission recommends maintaining the current postal monopoly over written, personal and business mail correspondence, and preserving sole Postal Service access to customer mailboxes. However, the President's Commission envisions giving the Postal Regulatory Board the duty to clarify and review periodically the scope of the monopoly and sole access to mailboxes. Most importantly, the President's Commission would transfer the power to redefine the monopoly to the Postal Regulatory Board.

Over time, the President's Commission foresees a gradual narrowing of the monopoly with a corresponding opening up for private businesses. This is a worthy goal that, in many ways, will increase access to innovative, efficient alternative service providers. I have one important concern about a shrinking monopoly, however. The President's Commission recommended a full set of interdependent recommendations. The shrinking of the monopoly, in particular, is highly dependent on dramatic new opportunities to reduce postal costs. If the efficiencies and cost reductions predicted by the President's Commission are not realized, then I fear that a shrinking monopoly will put increasing pressure on those captive mailers who remain in the monopoly to fund the universal service obligation. In other words, as a growing amount of postal volume is no longer subject to the monopoly, the captive customer volume subject to the monopoly becomes smaller. If costs do not experience a corresponding reduction, then those fewer mailers who are still subject to the monopoly (e.g., citizens of rural communities) will have to bear a higher cost per piece. I would ask this distinguished Committee to prevent such a result.

New Approach to Setting Rates

The President's Commission recommends dramatic changes to the system of changing rates. The newly established Postal Regulatory Board would construct a framework for rate increases along new lines.

Non-competitive products. Rates for non-competitive products – identified as First-Class Mail, Standard Mail, Periodical Mail, Media Mail, Library Mail, and Bound Printed Matter – will be set initially in a baseline rate case, probably applying the current pricing criteria of the Postal Reorganization Act. In view of the fact that First-Class Mail, Media Mail, and Library Mail are all heavily used by consumers and small businesses, I ask the distinguished Committee to provide explicitly for protection of these interests by a consumer representative, possibly the Office of the Consumer Advocate.

As part of the baseline case, the Postal Regulatory Board will devise an incentive-based scheme for non-competitive rates to rise, largely at the discretion of the Postal Service. The President's Commission envisions an escalator that will be comprised of an inflation factor that will allow the rates to rise, but with a productivity deflator that will moderate the inflationary impact. The President's Commission expects that the established rate ceilings will drive postal management in the direction of controlling costs and realizing new efficiencies, both laudable objectives. In addition, current Postal Reorganization Act-style rate hearings will be supplanted by highly streamlined new procedures that will give postal management the ability to increase rates within a small fraction of the current length of time expended in an omnibus rate case.

One scenario that is not specifically considered by the President's Commission is that the incremental costs of a particular non-competitive product may rise even faster than the escalator allows. Eventually the costs of the non-competitive product may exceed its revenues, and the deficit might grow even larger over time. I recommend that provision be made for an emergency rate request by the Postal Service to the Postal Regulatory Board to increase rates to a level that would cover the costs of the non-competitive

Allen Sanford GOING POSTAL

Senate Committee on Homeland Security and Governmental Affairs   Page 6 of 10

product. If this correction is not made, then other non-competitive products might be forced to cross-subsidize the deficient non-competitive product, a condition that the President's Commission has found to be uneconomic and undesirable.

From time to time, the Postal Service may find that its costs have increased above the aggregate level of revenues allowed under the non-competitive product escalator. In such cases, the President's Commission recommends an advance review by the Postal Regulatory Board of rate increases proposed by the Postal Service. It is not clear whether such requests must be granted. Under the current Postal Reorganization Act, following a request by the Postal Service, the Postal Rate Commission must always recommend rate increases for specific mail classes to be high enough to allow the Postal Service to break even. Would this still be the case after postal reform? As before, I recommend statutorily designated representation of consumer and small business interests.

Due Process in Postal Regulatory Board Proceedings. When rate increase cases take place before the Postal Regulatory Board, it is imperative that mailers who will be subject to rate increases be accorded full due process. Under the Postal Reorganization Act, requests by the Postal Service to increase rates or add new classifications are conducted under the provisions of the Administrative Procedure Act. Although the President's Commission does not raise the matter of due process, almost certainly this distinguished Committee will want to carry over the former due process guarantees from the Postal Reorganization Act into postal reform legislation. If that is the case, it is doubtful that the sixty-day proceedings recommended by the President's Commission can furnish due process to those who will be disadvantaged by Postal Service actions.

The Administrative Procedure Act requires agencies such as the Postal Regulatory Board to give all interested litigants the opportunity for submission of documentary or oral direct evidence, rebuttal evidence, cross-examination, and the submission of arguments. Furthermore, in most cases involving postal rate increases, the Postal Service will be in sole possession of much of the material needed to dispute the Postal Service's request. Opponents of the Postal Service's position will need sufficient time to obtain this information through discovery. Once the record has been fully developed by the litigants, and arguments have been submitted, the Commission will then need time to consider the parties' evidentiary presentations and arguments. Completion of all of these essential procedural activities will require more than the sixty days recommended by the President's Commission. Rushing through a case in sixty days is likely to result in a denial of due process.

If the Postal Regulatory Board is given strong, comprehensive powers to require the collection and reporting of financial data necessary for an evaluation of the request for additional revenues, and these data are filed regularly with the Board, it may be possible to make some reduction in the length of time for a request for rate increases above and beyond the established price cap. This truncation of the rate increase proceeding may avert a denial of due process to litigants only if the Board, and the public, are kept fully and currently informed about the Postal Service's financial position. The only reason that it may be possible to make some reduction in the length of time for Postal Regulatory Board proceedings, as compared to Postal Rate Commission proceedings, is that the public availability of relevant data should shorten the time needed both by the Postal Service to prepare requests and by mailers to evaluate them. Nevertheless, it is impossible to imagine that due process can be fully accorded litigants in sixty days. I am confident that this distinguished Committee can strike the proper balance between providing additional revenues quickly for the Postal Service while preserving due process for those mailers who will be faced with the imposition of higher rates.

Competitive products. Competitive products would include the current postal products of Express Mail, Priority Mail, and Parcel Post. (It is unclear whether Standard Mail packages, i.e., those less than 16 ounces, would be in the competitive or noncompetitive group). Changes in the rates of competitive products should be made at the discretion of the Postal Service, according to the President's Commission. The Postal Regulatory Board, however, would be charged with ensuring that aggregate non-competitive products do not cross-subsidize competitive products and that individual non-competitive and competitive products are not being cross-subsidized by other, non-competitive products. Furthermore, competitive products should be required to make a meaningful contribution toward overhead.

http://www.senate.gov/~gov_affairs/index.cfm?Fuseaction=Hearings.Testimony&HearingI... 5/24/2007

41

A complaint mechanism would provide for the filing of complaints from members of the public on the grounds that the rate of a non-competitive product exceeds its ceiling or that a competitive product is being cross-subsidized. To protect captive customers, the complaint procedure should also be available to those who have reason to believe that particular non-competitive products are being cross-subsidized by other non-competitive products. Consistent with my earlier suggestions, I would include a statutory provision authorizing a consumer representative to lodge such complaints. In addition, I would ask that this distinguished Committee establish a timeframe for such proceedings that ensures full due process to the litigants.

Cost Allocation. The President's Commission recommends that the Postal Regulatory Board take strong measures to ensure thorough, accurate cost allocation. One of the key tools for obtaining such information is subpoena power for the Postal Regulatory Board. Subpoenas are necessarily available only for information that the Postal Service has previously collected. Unless specific, this power may not always ensure that all of the information necessary to allocate costs appropriately will be collected. I am of the opinion that Congress should confer explicitly on the Postal Regulatory Board the power to establish rules for the collection and reporting of the type of information required to discharge the allocation duty effectively.

In addition, the President's Commission urges the Postal Service to comply voluntarily with Securities and Exchange Commission ("SEC") reporting requirements. There are two distinct virtues of such voluntary compliance: 1) SEC reporting is well understood by the public, and 2) SEC reporting allows a ready comparison between the Postal Service's financial reports and those in the private sector. However, the Postal Regulatory Board should not be limited to SEC documents to fulfill its mission. It must have authority to require periodic reporting of needed data to meet the abbreviated timelines suggested by the President's Commission.

Retained Earnings. The President's Commission recommends that the Postal Service be permitted to retain earnings up to a limit established by the Postal Regulatory Board. The President's Commission contemplates the accrual of retained earnings both from non-competitive and competitive products. The ability to retain earnings will reduce the need for management to seek emergency rate increases. Only after exhausting retained earnings could management justify an emergency rate increase.

Service Standards and Performance. Forces such as declining First-Class volumes, a narrowed monopoly, and price caps may combine to put the Postal Service in a position that makes it difficult for the Postal Service to meet established service standards. The natural tendency of any monopoly service provider in straitened circumstances is to allow its performance to deteriorate. ➡ |||

While the President's Commission recommends a mechanism for Postal Regulatory Board review of sweeping national changes in service standards, it does not propose a role for the Postal Regulatory Board to establish service standards for postal non-competitive products, require specified levels of performance, require the Postal Service to measure performance, and finally, require the Postal Service to submit the performance metrics to ➡ ||| the Postal Regulatory Board for public dissemination. These powers should be granted the Postal Regulatory Board in order to ensure that the public has the level of postal services it needs.

I further request that a consumer representative, designated by statute, also be given a role in defining service standards to meet consumer needs. The consumer representative should be given the additional power to lodge complaints about service when the metrics show that performance has fallen below Postal Regulatory Board standards. Postal Regulatory Board powers and consumer representation are imperative to ensure high quality services by a monopoly provider like the Postal Service. When, by law, the Postal Service is the only entity empowered to provide personal and business correspondence services, it can risk a serious deterioration in quality of service because it can count on retaining most of its monopoly volume.

Service Standards and Performance for Noncompetitive Products. The best method for ensuring adequate service standards and high levels of performance is to give the Postal

Allen Sanford   GOING POSTAL

Regulatory Board the power to: (1) define and establish service standards for non-competitive products, (2) set minimum performance requirements, (3) require the Postal Service to measure its performance, (4) require the Postal Service to report the performance results to the Postal Regulatory Board, and (5) give the Postal Regulatory Board the power to initiate its own investigation of service and performance issues. These powers should be augmented by the power to subpoena any records in the possession of the Postal Service that are relevant to these measurements.

This is why there was a fire!!

A model for the establishment of such service standards and measures may be found in the Postal Directive of the European Union. Under the directive, 85% of cross-border letter mail must be delivered in three days, and 97% must be delivered in five days.

At the present time, the Postal Service collects and reports performance information on First Class through two major data collection efforts: the Origin Destination Information System ("ODIS") and the External First Class measurement system ("EXFC"). ODIS data are filed regularly with the Postal Rate Commission under the Commission's rules. The Commission makes these data available to the public at its website. EXFC has a limited release by the Postal Service. Both of these data systems collect mail statistics chiefly on collection box mail, and the Postal Service is to be commended for doing so.

In the Oakland Office earlier this year!!

The Postal Service has elected not to collect information on much of the bulk business mail that it handles, including bulk First Class and Standard Mail, and Periodicals; I am the recipient of weekly e-mailed reports of a planet-code tracking company called Mail Trak. Mail Trak collects the tracking information made available from Postal Service barcode readers at Processing and Distribution Center facilities through a new service called Confirm that the Postal Service offers. Purchasers of Confirm service, generally bulk First-Class Mailers and Standard Mailers, use the Mail Trak company to collect tracking information and relay it to them in a user-friendly form. Mail Trak aggregates performance information from its customers and distributes the aggregate results in a weekly newsletter. In the past year, Mail Trak reports that approximately 23% of Standard Mail letters were being delivered later than the service standard window of 7 – 10 days. This is valuable information that Mail Trak is able to provide only for its customers' mailings. The Postal Service, on the other hand, could collect and report tracking information for all postal Confirm customers. A Postal Regulatory Board power to require such collection and reporting could make important performance information available to the Postal Service's Standard Mail (and bulk First Class) customers.

Here is !! the scam is : where they !!

The Postal Service does not regularly collect or report information on special services that are ancillary to the provision of non-competitive postal services like First Class. Certified Mail with Return Receipt serves as an important example. The Postal Service does not collect information on the percentage of Certified Mail pieces that actually carry the recipient's signature – the key feature of the service. In the case of Return Receipts, the Postal Service does not measure and report the average length of time for Return Receipt cards to be mailed to the recipient; and the Postal Service does not measure the percentage of such cards actually returned to recipients. These are the essential features of the service being purchased, but the purchaser does not have a clear idea of how often the promised service is actually provided. The Postal Regulatory Board should be given the power to define the essential elements (or service standards) for each special service ancillary to non-competitive products, to require measurement of the performance of the service standard, require submission of the data collected, and to disseminate the performance results to the public.

Performance of the Universal Service Obligation. Other types of information relating to the universal service obligation should also be required of the Postal Service through the Postal Regulatory Board. Examples of this type of information are the length of time a typical mailer waits on line at a retail facility, how quickly a postal agent responds to a complaint, the number and placement of collection boxes in a community, the frequency of collection and collection times for such boxes, and the hours for access to services at postal retail facilities and alternative access in other retail businesses.

Defining service standards and minimal service performance levels should be added to the Postal Regulatory Board's powers to prevent service deterioration from becoming a recourse against declining volumes and growing pressure to reduce costs. Since the Postal Service will have a statutory monopoly on most of the noncompetitive mailpieces,

43

the only way to ensure high quality performance is to have it regulated by the Postal Regulatory Board.

Service Quality for Competitive Products. In general, the Postal Regulatory Board will have no role in defining or monitoring quality of service for competitive products. The Postal Service is expected to compete in the marketplace on quality as well as price. However, the competitive playing field should be level with respect to false advertising claims. The private companies with which the Postal Service will compete will be subject to Federal Trade Commission ("FTC") laws and regulations prohibiting false advertising of products. Since the Postal Service will be acting as an ordinary business (not a governmental entity) in providing competitive products, it should be subject to FTC jurisdiction and to the same laws and regulations as other businesses.
Antitrust Laws. The reasoning set forth in the preceding paragraph applies with equal force to antitrust law and regulation. Although the Postal Service will be prevented from cross-subsidizing competitive products under the President's Commission formulation, there is a broad range of anticompetitive activity that is not related to cross-subsidy that the Postal Service may be free to engage in. I respectfully ask that this distinguished Committee give serious consideration to making the Postal Service subject to antitrust laws with respect to competitive products.

Postal Insurance. This distinguished Committee may want to address separately the Postal Service's sale of insurance as a service ancillary to the sale of competitive products such as Priority Mail and Parcel Post. Insurance sales by the Postal Service's competitors will be subject to any state laws requiring shippers to provide minimal information on the nature of the insurance contract. There may be regulation by state insurance commissions of the terms and conditions of package insurance. Furthermore, courts will likely apply ordinary contract law in disputes between purchasers of insurance and the private shippers insuring their packages.

The Postal Service as a governmental entity under current laws is exempt from all of the regulations and limitations described above. In disputes between the Postal Service and its claimants, courts have held that the Postal Service is essentially self-regulating, i.e., it writes its own regulations limiting its obligation under the insurance contract and it applies and interprets these rules when insurance purchasers submit claims. In court proceedings, the Postal Service enjoys a burden of proof standard much less onerous than its competitors. In a case involving a private shipper as defendant, the plaintiff will be required to prove his or her case by slightly more convincing evidence than that submitted by the defendant. In a case involving the Postal Service as defendant, the Postal Service's decision to deny an insurance claim will be upheld unless it is "plainly in error" or "clearly erroneous." This imposes a much higher burden of proof on plaintiffs of postal claims.

I would ask that the playing field between the Postal Service and its shipping competitors be leveled with respect to insurance and that the interests of postal insurance purchasers be protected.

Conclusion

In conclusion, I would like to give the President's Commission the highest praise for mastering a massive amount of technical material on the Postal Service's operations, cost structure, main sources of revenue, and the system of ratemaking used at the Postal Rate Commission. The recommendations made have obviously been reached after thoughtful, careful deliberation. I ask that the President's Commission recommendations be incorporated into postal reform legislation along the lines that I have suggested in my testimony. I thank the distinguished Committee for this opportunity to testify.

———

1 The United States Postal Service (1973 ed., Praeger Publishers) at pages 196 – 199.

The Postal Service did not pay any attention to Ms. Dreifuss. The "Forever Stamp", will make things more ambiguous and public input will continue to be ignored.

Who will benefit if the Postal Service makes performance information more ambiguous? The people who make the postal equipment, the people who make the components for the equipment, marketing companies, and direct mailers. Let use not forget the energy company, and last but not least, Postmaster John Potter and the "Good Old Boy's Club," that is relying on continued rate increases to insure that they continue to get cost of living and pay for "economic value added."

The Postal Service operates a network of approximately 275 major mail Processing and Distribution Centers (P & DCs) that serve as the interface between local post offices and the rest of the nation. A medium-sized P & DC might receive as many as 5,000,000 letters, 500,000 flats, and thousands of parcels (even though they scrap the equipment prematurely). Advanced equipment in the form of optical character readers, automated facer cancellers, bar-code sorters, and material handling systems have as much of the mail stream as possible. Approximately 95% of the letters and flats are sequenced automatically in the order in which they will be delivered. 23% of this mail is not delivered in a timely manner. This is according to a company that is employed by the Postal Service. I think that it should be more like 40% if you consider the mail that is sent to "nobody," or says to occupant or was sent to someone who lived there before or someone who happens to be dead.

Look at your mail. On a normal day you will get at least one letter addressed to "Occupant," or addressed to someone once who lived at the address. This is mail that the Postal Service has been paid for delivering. It has been processed until the mail volume numbers are where the P & DC want them then it is sent to you. Ask your carrier to stop delivering it. He will tell you to just throw it away. Pay attention!

Mail to my mother ... She died in 1994

Who takes the loss when ambiguity is the norm? People who publish magazines? Small time mailers or You and I?

46

Where is the representation for the average guy, the small business man and the magazine publisher? Where was the Union, E.E.O. the Senate, the Congress, the Office of Special Council, the F.B.I and the OIG's office that was determined to root out "fraud, waste, abuse and mismanagement? I've contacted all of them. Their reactions should interest you. (I have some letters at the end of the book).

Ever since President Lyndon B. Johnson appointed a commission to re-organize the Post *Office* on "a business basis" in 1967, the postal system has become frozen into a defensive posture, tied down in a manner akin to Gulliver in his travels by demands from such groups as major corporate mailers, competitive rivals, and partisan politicos.

There has been no place for bold new ventures of the past, such as Rural Free Delivery, Parcel Post, Postal Savings, Air Mail, or even the ambitious, yet fruit-less, Missile Mail experiment of the 1950s. If the Post Office department had been responding to the profit-making demands of the market, or to the po-litical influence of large corporations, none of these advances would have been attempted. Parcel Post, lest we forget, was introduced in the face of corporate competitors' opposition due to the fact that they were providing entirely unsatis-factory, oftentimes price-gouging, service to parts of the nation.

President Ronald Reagan called government "the problem". Was govern-ment the problem when the Post Office made open communication between the Continental Congress and George Washington's army possible during the Revolutionary War? Was government the problem when the Post Office pro-vided invaluable aide to the establishment of a vibrant national and local press by delivering periodicals throughout the land? How about when the Post Office Department constructed a national infrastructure for aviation? Is government the problem when letters and packages from home reach servicemen in distant parts of the world today? Or when citizen organizations are enabled or often made possible by a non-profit postage rate?"...

"Absence of an understanding of the Postal Service as a public service has al-lowed corporatists to obscure our postal system's defining mission; 'to bind the nation together'. There are promoters of a corporate postal system who would ultimately like to steal the Postal Service from the American people by eliminat-ing its public service function and privatizing (i.e. corporatizing) it. Operation of the postal system on 'a business basis' has helped make their case for them."

"Instead of focusing on new ways for our government to serve its citizens through the Postal Service, service reductions- such as closing post offices, removing collection boxes, and ending door delivery- have shifted emphasis to business practices focusing on how much the traffic will bear, further diminishing the spirit of the public service."

"A recent push for postal 'reform' legislation demonstrates the degree to which the public has been marginalized. Postal Service management, major mailers, corporate ideologues, business competitors, postmaster associations and the beleaguered postal unions have all been included in this legislative process, but there has been a noticeable absence- the consumer, who has been excluded from having a seat at the table. The bills which have gone through Congress reflect this absence. Instead of being discarded, as they largely should have been, the recommendations of the recent corporate dominated President's Commission on the Postal Service, which were not public service oriented, are apparent in the legislation."...

These quotes are from Ralph Nader. It is taken from his introduction to "Preserving the People's Post Office," by Christopher W. Shaw.

There was a period in the 70's and 80's when the Union was winning a lot of grievances. Sexual harassment and fraud were the primary cases that were won.

There was a case in which fraud and sexual harassment occurred. The manager could not gain sexual favors from the employee. The manager bypassed the employee for promotion to supervisor saying that the position was abolished. The manager had exposed himself to the employee. This alone would not have won the case because it was done in private it would be his word against hers. This manager however had a history of doing this. The Postal Service just moved him from place to place to cover up his actions.

The fraud is what got him. Custodial bids can't be abolished unless there is a reduction in the building square footage. This had not occurred. In addition a male employee was promoted to the position. Needless to say this manager was toast.

In another case an employee passed out and fell to the floor. The manager declared that he was drunk and had him taken home by a fellow employee. It turned out that the employee had a stroke. This employee remains incapacitated to this day. His wife who was also a Postal worker had to leave her job to take care of him. The Postal Service, E.E.O. and Workman's Compensation fought for four years to keep from paying. It was a severe hardship on this family and it all began because the manager would not file the CA-1 (accident claim form).

This man was declared to be drunk by the supervisor who refused to file an accident report. This took three years and his wife had to quit her job as a postal employee to take care of him.

MIKE WATSON & ASSOCIATES INC.

P.O. Box 42158 • Portland, OR 97242-0158 • (503) 654-2334 • TDD (503) 654-2438

January 4, 1991

This is a case I worked on where the supervisor refused to fill out the proper paperwork. CA-1 or CA-2

Even Sleepin with this!!

IO
te 656

Re: Candido Suazo

CLAIM FINALLY ACCEPTED
SUBARACHNOID HEMORRHAGE FROM
RUPTURED CEREBRAL ANEURYSM

Dear Tom:

On November 18, 1988, your member, Candido Suazo, suffered a ruptured cerebral aneurysm, with serious complications. Surgery was performed and, as the result of such, he is physically unable to care for himself and has been totally disabled since November 18, 1988. He is not expected to ever be able to return to work.

Candido's wife, Stella, who is a mail handler for the Postal Service, could not find a qualified individual to assist her with her husband's condition and claim, so she filed a CA-1 form and submitted what information she could. Therefore, a claim was created by OWCP and a file number was issued.

Due to all of the paperwork involved and the constant requests for additional documentation from OWCP, Stella contacted me in hopes that I might be able to assist her husband, who is an APWU member, with his claim.

After reviewing the documentation that Stella sent, I realized that the CA-1 form she filed was incorrect for this type of condition. I had her fill out a CA-2, obtained the proper statement relating to job duties and the stress relating to such, and we submitted such directly to OWCP. In turn, OWCP then started handling the claim as an occupational condition rather than a traumatic injury. I was also able to obtain a new medical report from Candido's neurosurgeon, which I immediately submitted to OWCP.

On June 8, 1989, OWCP formally denied Candido's condition as being job related. Based on this, I requested an oral hearing on his behalf right away.

On April 11, 1990, the oral hearing was held. On May 21, 1990, the hearing officer's written decision was issued, which was negative.

GOULD 142-C

Allen Sanford   GOING POSTAL

Based on the hearing decision, I obtained an in-depth medical report
from a psychiatrist. With this report, I requested reconsideration
on July 13, 1990.

On August 13, 1990, the San Francisco OWCP denied my request for
reocnsideration.

In my opinion, I felt that the neurosurgeon had properly related to
all of the issues, and I also felt that the psychiatrist had related
to all of the psychological issues involved. Both doctors had shown
causal relationship. Based on this, I requested another
reconsideration on September 13, 1990, this time basing my request
on fact of law and procedural errors.

On December 21, 1990, the San Francisco OWCP issued a decision
pertaining to my request for reconsideration, accepting Candido's
claim.

I cannot tell you the time I have spent on this case. If OWCP (not
to mention the hearing officer) had reviewed the proper issues in
the very beginning, it would not have dragged on this long.

The Suazos have suffered financially, as well as emotionally. Now,
having the claim accepted, they are entitled to all federal
benefits, including time loss compensation retroactive to November
18, 1988.

This claim is not through yet, for there are still numerous loose
ends that must be tied up.

I am sorry for the length of this report. Believe me, if I had
related to everything that occurred, it would have taken one of my
famous novels.

As always, if you should have any questions, please contact me.

                        Yours in union solidarity,

                        mike

                        Michael J. Watson
                        President
MJW/ce

cc: Raydell R. Moore, Western Region Coordinator, APWU
     William P. Simms, State President, California APWU

The people won the case but the manager was never held accountable for his
actions and the Postal Service can't be sued because of his actions

In a case that was a good example of what was going on across the country, another employee who was up for promotion and on the promotion register was told that there were no positions available. He was however on detail to the job that he would eventually be promoted to, and had been for almost two years. Upon investigation it was found that not only was the position available, there were ten positions available. Once this was discovered and revealed the man was promoted. The employee was not given any back pay. This was being done across the country. As machines were brought, in lower level maintenance positions were abolished illegally, and people were required to do higher level work under threat of termination even if the work was life threatening, like it was for the man who was nearly electrocuted.

STEP 2
GRIEVANCE
APPEAL FORM — AMERICAN POSTAL WORKERS UNION, AFL-CIO

Exhibit #1

The grievance form (APWU Step 2 Grievance Appeal Form) filled in by hand.

12 DETAILED STATEMENT OF FACTS/CONTENTIONS OF THE GRIEVANT:

The grievant has and is being discriminated against in that he has been made to wait for promotion to level 5 mechanic for a year while casuals have been brought in to do level 5 work. The grievant has been required to train casuals to do level 5 work. There are currently two positions in the unit that should be vacated and two casuals doing level 5 work with power tools along with two other casuals who are performing work normaly done by level 5 mechanics.

13 CORRECTIVE ACTION REQUESTED: It is requested that a copy of the supervisor's Step 1 report, Form 2608, be mailed to the Union along with the Step 2 decision for this grievance.

The grievant should be promoted immediately retroactive to the date the casuals began work and he should be made. Positions # 00000001 and 2969527 made vacant and (2) two additional level 5 positions opened for bid.

Repeatedly he has been told that he has not been promoted because there are no positions.

Two employees have been placed on the PER ahead of Mr. Alcala on basis that they recieved a higher test score.

First, the union contends that level 5 General Mechanic positions are chosen by seniority not best qualified.

Second, the union contends that casuals have and are being used as "Relief" workers at Container Repair in lieu of promoting Mr. Alcala and Mr. Jones who have been on the PER now for 2 yrs.

Mr. Byrne was hired 10/93 he cannot be number one on a PER determined by seniority. Mr. Proffitt cannot be located on the current seniority list. Both men have been placed ahead of Mr. Alcala and Mr. Jones.

The long time that Mr. Alcala has been on detail demonstrates the need for a position. Also the fact that he has been required to train casuals to do maintenance craft work which should have been done by Mr. Jones, demonstrates the need for another position.

STEP 2 GRIEVANCE APPEAL FORM — AMERICAN POSTAL WORKERS UNION, AFL-CIO

1. DISCIPLINE (NATURE OF) — CONTRACT (ISSUE): *Art 38.6 - 3? E*   CRAFT: *Maint.*   DATE: *12-13-93*   UNION GRIEVANCE   USPS GRIEVANCE

2. TO USPS STEP 2 DESIGNEE (NAME & TITLE): Labor Relations Representative   INSTALLATION/SEC. CEN./BMC: Oakland Main Ofc, 1675 - 7th St, 94615   PHONE: 874-8404

3. FROM: LOCAL UNION (NAME OF): Oakland Local APWU   ADDRESS: 7700 Edgewater Dr., #656   CITY: Oakland   STATE: CA   ZIP: 94621

4. STEP 2 AUTHORIZED UNION REP. - (NAME & TITLE): *Allen J. Sanford Shop Steward CRC*   PHONE (OFFICE): 635-8497   PHONE (OTHER): 635-8498

5. LOCAL UNION PRESIDENT: Tom Beardsley   PHONE (OFFICE): 635-8497   PHONE (OTHER): 635-8498

STEP 1 MEETING & DECISION

6. WHERE - WHEN: UNIT/SEC/BR/STA/OFC: *CRC*   DATE/TIME: *12/3/93*   USPS REP./SUPR: *Phillips*   GRIEVANT AND/OR STEWARD: MET WITH

7. STEP 1 DECISION BY (NAME & TITLE): *Denied*   DATE & TIME: *12/3/93*   INITIALS   INITIALING ONLY DATE OF DECISION

8. GRIEVANT PERSON OR UNION: *Class Action — Training casuals for craft jobs*   ADDRESS   CITY   STATE   PHONE

9. SOCIAL SEC. NO.   SERVICE SENIORITY CRAFT (FTR - PTR - PTF):   LEVEL   STEP   DUTY HRS: # OF DAYS: SA SU M T W T F

10. JOB#/PAY LOCATION UNIT/SEC/BR/STA/OFC): *787*   OTHER INFORMATION   LIFETIME SECURITY   VETERAN YES☐ NO☐ YES☐ NO☐

11. Pursuant to Article XV of the National Agreement we hereby appeal to Step 2 the following Grievance alleging a Violation (but not limited to) the following: NATIONAL (Art.'Sec.)   LOCAL MEMO (ART./SEC.) OTHER MANUALS, POLICIES, LM MINUTES, ETC.

Article 7.1B, 8.8B, 1.5, 38.6, 38 E

12. DETAILED STATEMENT OF FACTS/CONTENTIONS OF THE GRIEVANT:
Roberto Alcala, Vincent Martinez, R. P. McGowan and Frank Banks have been training casuals to do maintenance craft work. Article 38.6A clearly addresses this issue in informing management as to who is eligable to be trained.

13. CORRECTIVE ACTION REQUESTED; It is requested that a copy of the supervisor's Step 1 report, Form 2608, be mailed to the Union along with the Step 2 decision for this grievance.

Mr. Alcala's seniority date, when he is promoted, should be retroactive to 11-30-93 and Mr. Alcala, Mr. Martinez, Mr. McGowan and Mr. Banks be paid at the rate of MPE 7 for the month of Dec. which is when the training occurred. Allen J. Sanford CRC.

June 1996 15

USPS Attacks on Jobs Continue

APWU Addresses Subcontracting

The APWU has learned that the Postal Service, in an unprecedented attack on the bargaining unit, has formed a committee at the highest level to determine ways to contract out more work. It has already been reported in the *APWU News Service* that the USPS intends to contract out the Priority Mail Centers. In addition to the thousands of clerk jobs that will be lost are many maintenance jobs that would have been needed to maintain the equipment used to sort priority mail.

This committee has also been charged with attempting to contract out the Mail Transport Equipment (MTE) Repair Centers. These centers repair all types of mail transport equipment such as hampers, sacks, over-the-road containers and other equipment used to move the mail.

For several years a pilot project, operated by contractors, has been in operation in Greensboro, NC. While most of the work is mailhandler work, about 20 maintenance jobs would have been created in an MTE repair center. The Postal Service expects to create at least 20 of these centers across the nation. Along with the work-rules leadership, Maintenance Division officers visited the facility in Greensboro. The employees there have not been well informed about this community sweatshop. Ex... for managers, there...

manual labor in a building with no air conditioning and a welding area that contributed to the heat. Employees were observed six feet apart, but no conversation was taking place. When asked about this, the manager responded that the height of their production standards is set so that

employees don't have time to talk. And if employees don't meet the standards, they are fired, the manager said.

Cooperation?

Maintenance Division Director Jim Lingberg notes that, "We have seen in any number of publications that APWU refuses to cooperate with management—and I fail to understand what cooperation is. Can Mr. Runyon or Joe Mahon or any of their henchmen truly believe that this union is going to stand by and salute while our jobs are eliminated by contracting out? Do they truly believe that we would agree to set up sweatshop conditions that exist in the contractor-run MTE repair center?"

Lingberg, speaking on behalf of all the division officers, emphasizes, "This union has never cooperated in working condtions and we aren't about to start now. To do so would be to capitulate, not cooperate, and that ain't our style."

FSM 1000

In a recent letter to his managers, Rex Gallaher, the manager of the

Maintenance Technical Support Center (MTSC), advised that MPE mechanics were to remove defective personal computers from the flat sorting machine (FSM) 1000. After that, the MPE should then "trouble shoot" and repair the FSM, according to Gallaher. However, say the APWU officers, this work is covered by the electronic technician job description and should be performed by ETs. If any MPE is assigned to this work, they should immediately file a grievance requesting higher-level pay.

BMC and Maintenance Mechanic L-4

This same Rex Gallaher recently released to the field new preventive maintenance routes for the conveyor systems in the bulk mail centers. Included in these routes are minimum mechanics as the minimum level for some of the tasks. In accordance with the interim BMC staffing guidelines for the BMCs, the only mechanics in the BMCs should be levels 5, 6 or 7, say the officers. "The parties at this level agreed to these guidelines in 1979 and there has been no discussion regarding any changes. If level 4 MM jobs are created in your BMC," they say, "a grievance should be filed protesting the violation of the staffing guidelines. Additionally, grievances should be filed requesting higher-level pay for any level-4 maintenance mechanics that are created in your facility."

Casuals

The current "On Rolls/Paid Employee Statistics" (ORPES) report reflects that there are about 450 casuals in the maintenance craft nationwide. While there may be contractually proper reasons for some of these casuals, the division officers doubt that there is justification for 450. They ask: "Please review the staffing package for your facility. If your facility is below the authorized complement and there are casuals in the maintenance craft, process a grievance protesting a violation of Article 7. As a remedy request that the career employees be recalled [or all hours worked by the casual hired in...]"

UNITED STATES POST OFFICE
<u>RECEIVEL</u>

DATE: April 6, 1994   APR 1 2 1994

OUR REF: JREEL:hh:94615-9343:g-275-94,jr   Oakland APWU

SUBJECT: Step 2 Grievance Decision

                                    Installation: Oakland P&D C
                              • Installation Finance #05-5509
TO: • ALLEN SANFORD   Grievant's Name: Roberto Alcala
           SHOP STEWARD   ·   Grievant's SSN: 563-04-1722
           APWU OAKLAND LOCAL   Incident Date: 01-11-94
           7700 EDGEWATER DR #656   Local Union Grievance #MA038-94
           OAKLAND CA 94621   Local Management Grievance #G-275-!

Receipt is acknowledged of a Step 2 standard grievance form
submitted by you wherein you allege management is in violation of
Article 38 of the National Agreement. As a result, a Step 2
discussion was held between Kelley Plumb and me on March 8, 1994.

After careful review of the facts in this case and based on the
particular circumstances, this grievance is denied. The reasons
for my decision are as follows:

Casual employees are used as submittal workforce to offset
employees on extended leave, pending removal action or seasonal
activities. Management reserves the right to use casuals (Article
7, National Agreement). The aforementioned employee Robert Alcala
was not promoted because no <u>vacant</u> duty assignment was available.
See Article 38, Section 4.

JOSEPH REEL
MANAGER MAINTENANCE OPERATIONS T-2
OAKLAND P & D CENTER
US POSTAL SERVICE
1675 7TH ST RM 244-1W
OAKLAND CA 94615-9343

[Handwritten annotations: "O.R.: See Attached. Info does not Match. Please reconcile. Thanks. Joyce" and "C. FRED Sette"]

To Maintenance Manager

Oakland P &DC
Craft Position Authorizations/Status

Mechanization/Automation LDC 36

	On Roll	Authorized levels			Vacancies	Position assignments				Comments
		Old	New	Difference		Tour I	Tour II	Tour III	CRC	
ET PS-10	1	1	1	0	0	0	0	1	0	
ET PS-09	50	70	78	4	14	23	30	25	0	
ET PS-08	14	10	10	0	0	1	6	3	0	
Maint Mech, MPE PS-07	17	19	21	2	4	13	4	4	0	
Maint Mech, MPE PS-06	20	24	23	0	7	13	6	4	2	
Welder PS-06	2	2	2	0	0	0	0	0	14	
Gen Mech, PS-05	11	15	15	0	4	0	0	0	0	
Mech Helper PS-04	2	3*	2	0	0	3	0	0	0	* 1 position reverted to Grp Ld
Subtotal:	117	148	152	6	29	53	46	37	16	

Plant Building Equipment and HMO LDC 37

	On Roll	Authorized levels			Vacancies	Position assignments				
		Old	New	Difference		Tour I	Tour II	Tour III	FMO	
Area Maint Tech PS-08	1	1	1	0	0	0	0	0	1	
Area Maint Spec PS-07	1	1	1	0	0	0	0	0	1	
Machinist PS-07	1	1	1	0	0	0	1	0	0	
Elevator Mech PS-07	4	4	4	0	0	0	4	0	0	
BEM Mech PS-07	2	3	3	0	1	2	6	2	3	
Engineman PS-06	11	15	15	0	5	0	2	0	5	
Electrician PS-06	4	4	4	0	0	0	2	0	2	
Postal Mach Mech PS-06	1	2	1	0	0	0	2	0	1	
Painter PS-06	2	2	2	0	0	0	3	0	0	
Carpenter PS-06	3	3	3	0	0	0	1	0	1	
Plumber PS-06	2	3	2	–	0	(1)	(1)	(1)	0	
Industrial Mech PS-06	1	1	0	0	0	0	0	0	0	
Welder PS-06	2	2	1	0	0	0	1	0	2	
Letter Box Mech PS-06	1	2	2	5	5	3	22	1	16	
Gen Mech PS-05			7					4		
Subtotal:	38	45	47	5	11	3	22	4	16	

Position assignments — ( ) Assignments of old positions

** ( ) Five (2) positions unassigned

Page 1

cd: craft
Updated 4-17-95

American Postal Workers Union, AFL-CIO

1300 L Street, NW, Washington, DC 20005

April 11, 1997

Idowu Balogun
National Business Agent
Maintenance Division
150 E. Colorado Blvd
Suite 208
Pasadena, CA 91105
(818) 585-1404
(818) 585-0091 FAX

A.J. Sanford
1134 Ward St.
Berkeley, CA 94702

Dear Mr. Sanford,

     I received your letter dated March 29, 1997 regarding grievance #MA379-96. I made the best possible settlement, (compensation of 10hrs to craft employees). I obtained this settlement in spite of the fact that there was not a single document attached to prove the alleged misconduct.

     There was no intent to embarrass you. You should not consider a Step 3 decision an embarrassment. <u>A Step 3 decision, like any other step decision should be seen as a decision between two neutral parties.</u>

     Regarding your request that all Maintenance Arbitration Certification for Oakland be sent to you, that information is sent directly to your local. I suggest you contact your local president for a copy.

     Thank you for your dedication to the American Postal Worker Union. Remember, it is not personal.

In Solidarity,

I. Balogun
National Business Agent
Maintenance Division

CC: Tom Beardsley
    President APWU, Oakland

IB;gc
Opeiu #2
(afl-cio)

National Executive Board
Moe Biller
President

William Burrus
Executive Vice President

Douglas C Holbrook
Secretary-Treasurer

Greg Bell
Industrial Relations Director

Robert L Tunstall
director, Clerk Division

James W. Lingberg
Director, Maintenance Division

Robert C Pritchard
Director, MVS Division

George N McKeithen
Director, SDM Division

Regional Coordinators
Leo F Persails
Central Region

Jim Burke
Eastern Region

Elizabeth "Liz" Powell
Northeast Region

Terry Stapleton
Southern Region

Rayded R Moore
Western Region

This doesn't sound like a warrior to me!! In Viet Nam he would not have lived very long

59

Article 25.*

pay. The failure of management to give a written order is no grounds for denial of higher level pay if the employee was otherwise directed to perform the duties.

Section 4. Higher Level Details

Detailing of employees to higher level bargaining unit work in each craft shall be from those eligible, qualified and available employees in each craft in the immediate work area in which the temporarily vacant higher level position exists. However, for details of an anticipated duration of one week (five working days within seven calendar days) or longer to those higher level craft positions enumerated in the craft Articles of this Agreement as being permanently filled on the basis of promotion of the senior qualified employee, the senior, qualified, eligible, available employee in the immediate work area in which the temporarily vacant higher level position exists shall be selected.

Section 5. Leave Pay

Leave pay for employees detailed to a higher level position will be administered in accordance with the following:

Employees working short term on a higher level assignment or detail will be entitled to approved sick and annual paid leave at the higher level rate for a period not to exceed three days.

Short term shall mean an employee has been on an assignment or detail to a higher level for a period of 29 consecutive work days or less at the time leave is taken and such assignment or detail to the higher level position is resumed upon return to work. All short term assignments or details will be automatically canceled if replacements are required for absent detailed employees.

131

Article 25.1

C. If the requested leave falls within the choice vacation period and the request is submitted after the determination of the choice vacation period schedule, the Employer will make every reasonable effort to grant such request, consistent with service needs.

(The preceding Article, Article 24, shall apply to Transitional Employees)

**ARTICLE 25
HIGHER LEVEL ASSIGNMENTS**

Section 1. Definitions

Higher level work is defined as an assignment to a ranked higher level position, whether or not such position has been authorized at the installation.

Section 2. Higher Level Pay

An employee who is detailed to higher level work shall be paid at the higher level for time actually spent on such job. An employee's higher level rate shall be determined as if promoted to the position. An employee temporarily assigned or detailed to a lower level position shall be paid at the employee's own rate.

(Additional provisions regarding Higher Level Pay for Transitional Employees can be found in Appendix A).

Section 3. Written Orders

Any employee detailed to higher level work shall be given a written management order, stating beginning and approximate termination, and directing the employee to perform the duties of the higher level position. Such written order shall be accepted as authorization for the higher level

130

Associated Press reported on October 4, 2007 that Wal-Mart had to pay workers back wages totaling $62.3 million on top of $78.5 million that was previously won. Wal-Mart was doing the same thing to these people that the Postal Service did. The Post Office however is protected by the Hatch Act Amendments and the fact that there is no Labor Relations Department.

A class action case against the Postal Service could never happen. The Postal Service owes thousands of people across the country higher level pay. Particularly, those people in maintenance department who were required to work in life threatening conditions.

The institution of the Hatch Act Amendments, the dismantling of the Labor Relations Departments and the E.E.O. section ensures that any class action against the Postal Service could not result in victory for the employees.

Managers know they are immune and it is reflected in their attitudes. The manager who lied when the worker was almost electrocuted did so with complete confidence, knowing that whatever was written would be taken at face value and he would not be questioned. This same manager tried to fire me early in my career but failed, because favoritism was shown to another employee with a record worse than mine. I was fortunate as there was a Labor Relations Department then.

Over the years this manager moved up through the ranks by playing on gender and race to divert attention away from incompetence. If the employee died as a result of his injury, she would have written the same letter to his family regretfully saying that the Postal Service didn't owe them the $200,000 for accidental death that he was entitled to. This would have happened even though the equipment should not have been in the building, and the man was not qualified to work on nor was he trained on the equipment.

This attitude is perpetrated and condoned by the IG. When a group of mechanics called the IG's office in Washington to complain about being forced to go to school to train to work on equipment that was obsolete, the response was "they can do that".

During this period, there were two brothers who were also managers in the maintenance department. Letters were written complaining about these two and petitions were circulated requesting that they be removed from the units they managed, if not flat out fired. The elder brother was deemed a snake by the union paper. He was so outraged that he took the union to court. After the union had presented its evidence the judge ruled in the Union's favor.

GOING POSTAL

Allen Sanford

This letter was written about the older brother of the supervisor about whom the petition was written.

26 November 1994

Mr. Ramon P. Yee
Electronic Technician (Tour I)
2613 Howland Court
Fairfield, Ca. 94533-1748

MR. FRED FLORANCE
SENIOR PLANT MANAGER
OAKLAND P & D CENTER
1675 7TH STREET
OAKLAND, CA. 94615

Anthony Butler's brother, Walter is also a manager. This letter was written in 94, since then Walter has recently been accused of contributing to a man's death by forcing him to remain at work after the man complained of illness.

Dear Sir:

I write to you with a sense of urgency, and only as a last resort.

My name is Ramon P. Yee. I'm an Electronic Technician (PS-09) on Tour I. I'm a father of four children, ages 7, 6, 2½ years, and a 5 month old baby. My wife is a full-time mother and housekeeper. I'm also a first-class petty officer Hospital Corpsman in the U.S. Navy Reserves.

I would like to bring to your attention and scrutiny a very disturbing work environment on Tour I (Maintenance and Engineering Support) that I feel will someday become "tragic." I refer specifically to the antics of one Mr. Walter Butler, Tour I MPE Supervisor (EAS-17). Mr. W. Butler has had numerous petitions and grievances filed against him from all the tours in maintenance. This man has been petitioned and grieved for actions deemed abusive and/or illegal. Records of these petitions and grievances are kept by several union shop stewards.

Mr. W. Butler's track record of abuses, harassments, intimidations, and malicious persecutions has cost the U.S. Postal Service irreparable harm in lost employees' morale and motivations. How much longer must we, the craft employees, endure this man's mockery of leadership? Mr. Walter Butler, as a manager, has no place in the future of the U.S. Postal Service.

Mr. WALTER BUTLER:

-Is grossly incompetent.
-Has a very limited knowledge of MPE work requirements.
-Does not know the correct complement of people needed to SAFELY perform work orders.
  -Has repeatedly assigned ONE PERSON on work orders where safety mandates a minimum of two people.
  -Has scheduled people on the work roster who were on their scheduled days off (not even on overtime), leaving areas undermanned, work orders dangerously understaffed.
  -Has refused to file a CA-1 (Accident Report) on behalf of Mr. Patrick Lucchesi, MPE Mechanic (PS-07).
    * A few weeks ago, Mr. Patrick Lucchesi was on a work order at the Monorail Sack Sorter when the Lift-A-Loft that he was on lost hydraulic pressure and came down suddenly. He immediately informed Mr. W. Butler about his accident and requested medical treatment. According to Mr. P. Lucchesi, Mr. W. Butler became angry and would not give a CA-1 form for him to fill out. Mr. P. Lucchesi went to the nurse's station for medical attention and had to call in sick the next day. Mr. P. Lucchesi claimed he was intimidated by Mr. W.

Butler, to the point that he never pursued to file a CA-1 report for his
accident.
-Has on several occasions reported late for work, sometimes as much as two hours.
If not for the initiative of individuals on our tour, time cards and route sheets
would not have gotten out to the various work crews.
-In my own case, has harassed and persecuted me for refusing to be an accomplice in
his attempts to fire a fellow employee. As reprisal for my refusal, I have
become your highest level janitor/custodian (PS-091). By this, I mean, that my
work assignments have been nothing more than dusting and cleaning. I wouldn't
mind this so much if all the ETs were rotated through these work assignments.
Unfortunately, I seem to be the only beneficiary of this treatment.
* I have been an Electronic Technician for almost two years now and have yet to
attend a qualifying ET school, or even train on our ET equipments. In the
meantime, newly-hired ETs are being sent to TTC, Norman, OK. for training. So
much for seniority in this organization.

Tour I maintenance management may claim inadequate manpower for lapses in equipment
coverages and upkeep, but the truth of the matter is that GROSS INCOMPETENCE, as
exemplified by supervisors such as Mr. Walter Butler, do more to erode the work forces'
initiative and enthusiasm, and far outweighs any and all excuses for people and
equipment failures.

There is danger in our situation on Tour I. Royce Harris, Manager, Maintenance Operations Tour I, has opted to let his supervisors handle all complaints. It's like
the proverbial fox guarding the chicken coop. Grievances are being filed through the
union and through EEO. I sincerely hope that no one ever resorts to violence but I
have to admit that tempers are up. Everyday at work people wonder who's next in line
for Mr. Walter Butler's harassments. It is quite a sight to see Mr. Walter Butler
walking through the building like a bully spoiling for a fight. Comments from him:
"I'm better than you, that's why I'm a level 17." makes us all shake our heads.

We have a problem on our tour that we, the work crews, deal with on a daily basis.
Here's hoping that this problem does not get any bigger.

Sincerely:

Ramon P. Yee
Mr. Ramon P. Yee
2613 Howland Court
Fairfield, Ca.   94533-1748

P.S.

I do not trust anybody on Tour I to give you a fair assessment of my character. To th:
end, I would like to name a couple of people who have known me for several years as
character references on my behalf.

Mr. LEON FRANCISCO   Capt. PATRICIA CHRISTMAN, NC, USNR
SENIOR MANAGER-OPERATIONS (T-2)   Director, Same-Day-Surgery Program
OAKLAND P&D CTR   TEL#(510) 798-6377(H)
                                                (510) 313-6213(W)

This man and his brother had the complete support of their superiors and
they were allowed to threaten people and falsify documents while pursuing action against an employee. These two are very lucky.

The elder brother would often brag about how he and his brother grew up on a farm under the strict hand of his father. He said he had it easy when he joined the military. He dealt with employees the way his father had dealt with him. He made a habit of telling people what they had better do. When he went to work in San Francisco, he put so much stress on one employee that the employee wrote his Congressman and was so convincing that he had to be suspended. It didn't do him any good. When he came back he got into it with another employee. Only this time the employee wasn't as diplomatic. My man got his clock cleaned in the parking lot.

His little brother is the one who made me aware of what was going on in the office. After I had filed the Safety Hazard Report regarding unsafe equipment, he made the comment, "I don't know why you are so worried about this equipment. We don't have to deliver that mail anyway."

It hit me right between the eyes. The only purpose for using this equipment was to store or hide the mail. After the employee was shocked while working on the equipment, the manager threatened to take action if he filed a accident report using accidents that he had in the past to put him on suspension. This was illegal.

This same man tried to do the same thing to me earlier. I hurt my back and he was upset that I demanded to file an accident report. If I had not filed that report and had my back examined it would not have been discovered that I had cancer. I had no signs of cancer. When the MRI was done on my back the doctor noticed something. He sent me for a blood test. I was lucky. Had I allowed myself to be intimidated I would be dead.

Explanation of the Hatch Act and Senator Boxer's Response. The Merit Systems Protection Board only responds if you have been terminated.

NAVIGATING THE HATCH ACT

In 1993, Federal and postal employees finally gained access to the political process when the Congress passed, and President Clinton signed into law, amendments to the Hatch Political Activities Act ("Hatch Act"). The original Hatch Act, first enacted in 1939 wanted to maintain neutrality and impartiality within the Civil Service by forbidding its involvement in political activities. The Hatch Act Reform Amendments now give federal and postal employees the right to participate in political activity as private citizens and protects their right to be free from improper political solicitation. However, the right to political participation has its own challenges. For the right to participate in political activity is not absolute. Despite many workshops and memoranda given by government agencies explaining the newfound rights of Federal and postal employees, employees are finding themselves before the Merit Systems Protection Board for violations of the Hatch Act. Below, is a discussion of the rights under the Amendments and why Federal employees must be vigilant to ensure that they are following all the proscriptions of the Hatch Act.

The Hatch Act Amendments apply to civilian federal employees, postal employees, part-time employees, D.C. government employees, special government employees and others who occasionally engage in government business. It does not cover the President, Vice President, General Accounting Office employees and members of the uniformed armed services or employees of security and crime prevention agencies. Generally, covered employees may actively participate in the management of political campaigns. However, this participation has clear defined limits. Also, permitted political can only occur under particular circumstances. First and foremost, Federal employees are prohibited from engaging in partisan political activities while on duty or on Federal property. This is called the "bright-line rule." When this bright-line rule and other restrictions are violated, the Amendments give the Office of Special Counsel ("OSC") the right to investigate and prosecute violations before the Merit Systems Protection Board. The OSC is aggressively enforcing this right.

Basically, Federal and postal employees can participate in the political process on their own time. They may: register and vote; be a candidate in nonpartisan elections; participate in political organizations; express opinions about candidates and issues; make a political contribution; attend and be active at political rallies and meetings; campaign for or against candidates in partisan elections;

distribute campaign literature; make campaign speeches for candidates in partisan elections; wear a button on a partisan political campaign when not on duty; and sign nominating positions. This list is not exhaustive, but it gives an idea of the activities that are permitted.

Hatch Act Amendments prohibitions include, but are not limited to: being a candidate for partisan political office; engaging in political activity on duty or in a government office or while wearing a official uniform; soliciting political contributions from the general public; using official authority or influence to interfere with an election; placing a partisan bumper sticker on a government vehicle; and wearing a button on a partisan political campaign while on duty or at a work site or wearing an official uniform.

Some cases prosecuted by the OSC illustrate the pitfalls of the Hatch Act Amendments. The OSC suspended a postal employee for thirty days after he ran as a partisan candidate in a school board election. The postal employee tried to circumvent the prohibitions of the Hatch Act by filing as both a Democrat and a Republican. The OSC ruled that filing as both a Democrat and a Republican does not negate the Hatch Act's prohibition against participation in a partisan campaign.

In another case, a federal employee took an extended leave to run for partisan political office. Again the OSC decided that such action was a violation of the Hatch Act.

Pitfalls are not only found in determining the partisan nature of a campaign and how to circumvent the prohibition against endorsing candidates. A federal employee was charged with violating the Hatch Act when he wrote a letter of endorsement, which included a request for contributions. An employee may not personally request, accept, or receive political contributions. However, the employee may solicit, accept or receive a political contribution from a person who is of the same federal labor organization or federal employee organization that has a multicandidate political committee.

The penalty under the act is removal from office or suspension of not less than thirty days. Removal would occur if circumstances show a deliberate disregard for the act. There continues to be a debate about whether the Act allows for debarment from federal employment. However, the Merit Systems Protection Board has determined that the act does not authorize debarment of employees removed for violation of the Hatch Act.

Federal and postal employees can protect themselves from prosecution for violating the Hatch Act by requesting an advisory opinion from the OSC. Inquiries can be made by phone, fax, mail or email to: Hatch Act Unit, U.S. Office of Special Counsel, 1730 M Street, N.W., Suite 300, Washington, D.C. 20036-4505; Telephone: (800) 854-2824, (202) 653-7143; Fax: (202) 653-5161; Email: hatchact@osc.gov.

BARA BOXER
CALIFORNIA

United States Senate
HART SENATE OFFICE BUILDING
SUITE 112
WASHINGTON, DC 20510-0504
(202) 224-3553
senator@boxer.senate.gov
http://boxer.senate.gov

COMMITTEES:
COMMERCE, SCIENCE
AND TRANSPORTATION
ENVIRONMENT
AND PUBLIC WORKS
FOREIGN RELATIONS

May 2, 2002

General Karla Corcoran
Inspector General
USPS Inspector Service
1735 North Lynn Street, # 10000
Arlington, VA 22209-2020

Dear General Corcoran:

Enclosed please find a copy of the correspondence Senator Boxer received from Mr. Allen J. Sanford, regarding difficulties he and other employees of the United States Postal Service have incurred under the management of Mr. Anthony Butler.

Due to the Hatch Act Reform Amendments of 1993, I understand that we are limited in the assistance we may be able to offer Mr. Sanford regarding personnel matters. However, I am forwarding the attached for your review and consideration. Any information you can provide in response to the concerns expressed by Mr. Sanford will be most appreciated.

Thank you in advance for your assistance in this matter. If you have any questions or require additional information, please feel free to contact Carla Jeanpierre at 415-403-0100.

Sincerely,

Eng J. Vizcaino
Director of Constituent Services

Enclosure
EJV/clj
cc: Mr. Allen J. Sanford

NTGOMERY STREET
SCO, CA 94111

□ 312 N. SPRING STREET
SUITE 1748
LOS ANGELES, CA 90012
(213) 894-5000

□ 501 T STREET
SUITE 7-600
SACRAMENTO, CA 95814
(916) 448-2787

□ 1130 'O' STREET
SUITE 2450
FRESNO, CA 93721
(559) 497-5109

□ 600 'B' STREET
SUITE 2240
SAN DIEGO, CA 92101
(619) 239-3884

□ 201 NORTH 'E' STREET
SUITE 210
SAN BERNARDINO, CA 92401
(909) 888-8525

Ms. Portia Munn   February 1, 2002
MMO USPS
1675 7ᵗʰ St RM 243W
Oakland, CA 94615

Ms Munn:

We, the undersigned, feel that Supervisor Anthony Butler should be removed as a Maintenance Craft Supervisor for the following reasons:

1. He has created a hostile and adversarial relationship with the mechanics, electronic technicians and other craft personnel in the maintenance department of the Oakland Processing and Distribution Center. This has been detrimental to the ability of us to perform our duties for the Postal Service and its customers.

2. His arrogance and confrontational manner have driven morale to an all time low and caused a stressful environment affecting employees both on the job and in their personal lives as well.

3. He treats his "subordinates" with disrespect. He refers to many loyal employees with decades of quality service to the Postal Service as "not acting like adults" and not performing their job assignments. We have been performing at high standards for years and, rather then being praised and rewarded, we are dishonored or punished.

4. He has tried to pit us against each other by implying that some jobs are more important than others, and favoring some individuals over others.

5. He is extremely vindictive, using his power over pay, job assignments and scheduling to "get even" with employees who in any way oppose or even question him.

6. Rather than dealing with particular individual problems, he issues sweeping edicts that are not appropriate to the group as a whole.

7. He hypocritically demands that his "subordinates" adhere to policies and rules that he himself does not follow.

8. He contends that mechanics, who for years have been performing their jobs satisfactorily, are now "not qualified" for the same jobs, and now must attend classes to meet his demands.

9. He does not listen to or follow the recommendations of his mechanics or electronic technicians as to the needs in order to adequately maintain the equipment.

10. He has been completely unwilling to address these grievances in order to mutually and cordially resolve them.

Please respond within 5 working days

cc:
Mr. A. Kirby Faciane	Mr. Robert Fisher	Mr. Royce Harris	Mr. Frederic Jacobs
DM USPS	SPM USPS	MM USPS	President APWU
1675 7ᵗʰ St RM 307	1675 7ᵗʰ St RM 236	1675 7ᵗʰ St RM 215	7700 Edgewater Suite 656
Oakland, CA 94615	Oakland, CA 94615	Oakland, CA 94615	Oakland, CA 94621

Respectfully,
The following Oakland P&DC maintenance employees :
Oakland P&DC
1675 7ᵗʰ ST RM 247w
Oakland, CA 94615

This is a copy of the petition that was circulated to have this supervisor removed from the unit. This is the same supervisor that tried to intimidate people into not filing accident reports.

These two individuals have been busted since my retirement. It seems that one brother signed a contract for the other brother to do some repair work at the station he managed. It seems that the amount of work done didn't correspond to the amount of money paid. Two birds were killed with one stone. I like it.

This is an extendable conveyor. It is suppose to assist in unloading and loading the trucks. It was being used to ram the mail into the truck as tight as possible then the van was left in the yard or on the street. They would break the machine everyday that is why I took the picture.

Until recently oil companies have been doing the same thing with oil that the Postal Service does with the mail.

Oil companies would buy oil for immediate delivery and stick it in their storage tanks, then sell contracts for future delivery at a higher price. When delivery dates neared, they closed out existing contracts and sold new ones for future delivery of the same oil. The oil never budged. The maneuver was known as the oil-storage trade.

BARBARA LEE
9TH DISTRICT, CALIFORNIA

COMMITTEES:
FINANCIAL SERVICES
Subcommittee on
Housing and Community Opportunity
Subcommittee on
International Monetary Policy and Trade

INTERNATIONAL RELATIONS
Subcommittee on Africa
Subcommittee on Europe

Congress of the United States
House of Representatives
Washington, D.C. 20515-0509

REPLY TO OFFICE CHECKED

☐ DISTRICT OFFICE
SANDRÉ R. SWANSON
CHIEF OF STAFF
1301 CLAY STREET, SUITE 1000N
OAKLAND, CA 94612
Phone: (510) 763-0370
Fax: (510) 763-6538

☐ WASHINGTON OFFICE
THOMAS C. McDANIELS, JR.
ADMINISTRATIVE ASSISTANT
426 CANNON H.O.B.
WASHINGTON, D.C. 20515
Phone: (202) 225-2661
Fax: (202) 225-9817

May 20, 2002

Mr. Kirby Faciane
District Manager
1675 -7th Street RM 304
Oakland. CA 94615

Dear Mr. Faciane:

My constituent, Mr. Allen Sanford, has requested my assistance regarding what he terms to be widespread "fraud, waste and mismanagement" that is occurring within the local Postal Service District.

Mr. Sanford has expressed his concern regarding the non-use and implementation of recently purchased Postal equipment. Mr. Sanford alleges that the Postal Service has yet to install these new machines and instead has opted to keep running the older outdated machines. Mr. Sanford also alleges that the management employees associated with negotiating and brokering the deal to acquire these machines received improper bonuses as a result of their involvement with the deal. In addition, Mr. Sanford claims that the work productivity records kept by the Postal Service are not properly maintained nor do they accurately reflect the true number of hours worked by Postal employees. In short, Mr. Sanford alleges that the books are "cooked." Enclosed please find information which explains the situation.

I would appreciate it if you would investigate and comment on these concerns at your earliest opportunity. Please forward your correspondence in care of my Staff Assistant, Mr. Adante Pointer, in my Oakland district office.

Thank you for your attention to this matter.

Sincerely,

Barbara Lee

Barbara Lee
Member of Congress

BL:am
Enclosure

PRINTED ON RECYCLED PAPER

Response from Congresswoman Barbara Lee. The district Manager had sent 2,000 pieces of equipment to Oakland from Los Angeles before he transferred to Oakland himself. Why would you leave L.A. to some to Oakland?

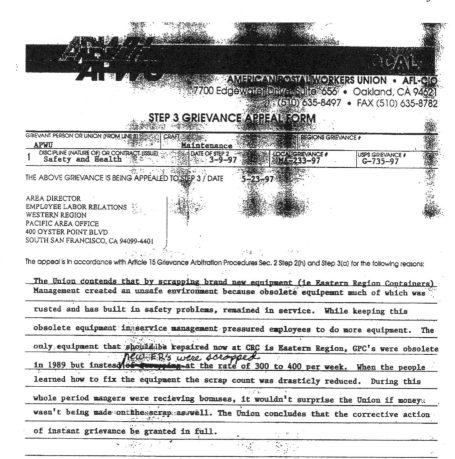

The grievance regarding the equipment that was being scrapped. It was ignored.

"The problem exist throughout the country." "Surveys have been taken
to determine where containers are LOST and from these surveys closed
loops can be developed to ensure the return of containers."(Page
116 of handbook PO-502 9/93).

The Union contends that management was aware of inventory control
problems,nation wide,for at least 3 years befor PO-502 was published. The
loops were never closed. Windows of opprotunity for fraud,waste and
mismanagement were opened wide. Had the MARS system not been implimen-
ted those windows would still be open.

Befor MARS, very sloppy records were being kept. There was no crosscheck or
quality control. Equipment surveys were stopped. Scrap committees were not
formed. Repair proceedures were not standardized. Employee suggestions
were kept local or not responded to.
There was no attempt by management to avoid additiopal cost.

Supervisors were rotated frequently and in Oakland,a 204B, with little
or no knowledge of maintenance or knowledge of the operation, was
allowed to remain in the unit fo a number of years.

In Oakland the sittuation degenerated to the point that the 204B was lending
employees money and allowing employees time on the clock to ride around
town and purchase drugs. These employees were EAP particapants and the
supervisor knew it.

The 204B was allowing these people to be put in a position to be busted
for drug sales and posession.

Agent Perez was assigned to CRC befor the two employees came into the unit.
The agent was in the unit to investigate theft. He could not find anything.

When the two victums came into the unit they were targeted imedeately.
The 204B in charge cooperated completly. He allowed the agent and the
employees time on the clock to party.

Why? Because the agent needed an excuse to be in the unit. Make two people
who have known drug problems backslide and then pin the theft on them.

The theft was not pinned on them in writing, but the investigation of
theft was stopped after the bust.

The agent would not have been in the unit were it not for comflaints of theft
made by a supervisor. The 204B was bringing a camera to work to cover himself.

Once the equipment became monitored by MARS, managment started useing
casuals. Management did not want to fill the positions. The staffing request
could not be justified based on the enventory on hand. Manhours were requested based on past staffing request.

On subsequent staffing request the depleted inventory numbers would be used
to justify exsessing the positions and the cost to replace the equipment
would be the excuse to contract out the jobs.

This effort to contract out CRC is clearly a case of planned obsolecence.
Supervisors who were unaware complained of theft and requested casuals based
on past quotas of casuals that had been allotted to the unit.

After 93 management failed to implement any of the guidlines set forth
in PO-502. Even after addmitting that inventory problems existed employees w
/were asked to produce more while working on equipment that was obsolete
and not given standardized proceedures for repairing the few remaining
pieces of equipment left in the system ie Eastern Region containers.
The Postal Service has a feduciary responsebility tothe public and the
employees.That responsebility has not benadhered to.

The UPS stike exposed the need for equipment.

The greivance should be granted in full and be forwarded to the IG.

OFFICE OF INSPECTOR GENERAL

UNITED STATES
POSTAL SERVICE

December 12, 1997

Mr. Allen J. Sanford
1134 Ward Street
Berkeley, CA 94702-2250

Dear Mr. Sanford:

[handwritten: Inflating + inven?]

This is in response to your undated letter, alleging that Postal Service management at the Oakland, California
Processing & Distribution Center is retaining obsolete, unsafe mail equipment while brand new equipment
remains in storage. In addition, you allege that the maintenance union business agent and Postal Service
management are in collusion, and that the business agent does not properly represent union employees.

[handwritten margin notes interspersed: Brand new equipment was scrapped first, once promotions and bonuses were recei... The old si... was kep... This means that they were aware that this was going on on the East Coast before I wrote this letter, I assume. This started in 92 nationwide.]

As information, the Inspector General, who is independent of postal management, is appointed by and reports
directly to nine Presidentially-appointed Governors of the Postal Service. The primary purpose of the Office
of Inspector General is to prevent, detect, and report fraud, waste, and program abuse, and to promote
efficiency in the operations of the Postal Service. The Office of Inspector General conducts independent
audits and investigations to ensure that Postal Service assets and resources are fully protected. It also has
oversight responsibility for all activities of the Postal Inspection Service. Further, the Inspector General helps
ensure that the Governors are kept fully aware of all emerging issues and significant events regarding postal
operations and programs.

The Postal Service attempts to resolve employment concerns informally through effective communication.
When this cannot be achieved, the grievance-arbitration procedures established under the National Agreement
between the Postal Service and the postal unions provide a forum for mediating disputes involving the
interpretation of rules, the perception of offensive behavior, or adverse management actions. These
procedures provide for an impartial hearing on these issues. Postal managers, as well as employees and their
representatives, are afforded ample opportunity to participate in the proceedings. The Inspector General fully
supports the grievance arbitration process as a viable means of resolving disputes similar to your own.

While the Office of Inspector General is very interested in labor-management issues, we do not routinely
investigate individual employee complaints. Our office performs postal-wide reviews to help promote a healthy
and productive work environment for all postal employees. Accordingly, we have formed review teams that will
consider issues, like those you raise, for possible systemic review. In this regard, we have referred your
correspondence to the appropriate Office of Inspector General Director for attention deemed warranted. You will
be contacted if additional details are required.

Thank you for writing the Office of Inspector General. Please refer to Postal Hotline Control #9700444 for future
inquiries concerning this matter.

Sincerely,

Jim H. Crumpacker
Security, Safety, and
Customer Concerns Division

475 L'ENFANT PLAZA SW
WASHINGTON DC 20260-0020
202-268-5600
FAX 202-268-5623

[handwritten: If this were true, based on the information that I submitted, a number of people should be in jail right now. Yet, people got bonuses and promotions and if you call this "Postal Hotline Control #9700444, wear an overcoat. It ain't hot!! Never was!! When did the level 25's get made in Oakland? Inventory was being retained to justify promotions and bonus...]

United States Postal Service **Grievance Summary - Step 1**	1. Grievant's Name (Last, First and Middle Initial) Class, Action APWU		
Forward the original of this form to your Step 2 Management Official. Complete items 1 through 12 and 21. If grievance is denied, complete items 13 through 20. If additional space is required, continue on reverse. See Handbook EL-921, Supervisor's Guide to Handling Grievances.			
2. Facility Container Repair Center	3. Craft Maintenance	4. Grievant's Title Maintenance Mechanic, Welder, Custodian	

5. Date of a. Incident 10/09/97 b. Step 1 Meeting 10/27/97
6. Was Grievance Timely at Step 1? [X] Yes [ ] No
7. Date of Step 1 Answer 10/27/97
8. Union Official A. Sanford

9. Issue (Complaint or Alleged Violation)
Union contends management is in violation of Articles 14 and 32 A&B. Proposal to contract CRC activities is a culmination of mismanagement which began in 1989.

10. Remedy Requested (Specify Requirements to Resolve Grievance)
Contracting out should be held in abeyance. All CRC positionss whould be upgraded to level PS 6 retroactive to 1992, in recognition of the efforts of the members of the unit. Two former emloyees should be re-enstated.

11. Decision (Check One) [ ] Sustained [ ] Settled [X] Denied [ ] Closed [ ] Withdrawn [ ] Other

12. Reasons for Decision
Union failed to substanciate any violation of health issues. Requested corrective actions for supposed violations are beyond authority of local management.

13. Grievance Data a. Level Varied b. Step Varied c. Tour 2 d. Section Maint e. Pay Location 787
14. Craft or Relevant Seniority Date Varied
15. Check One [X] FTR [ ] PTR [ ] PTF [ ] Rural Designation Code
16. Off Days S/S
17. Work Schedule 0650 - 1500

18. Background (State All Relevant Information And Attach All Supporting Documents)
Memo sent to CRC addressed the proposal to contract out CRC activities across the nation. An actural date of action is pending the performance results of pilot sites presently in operation back East. Until further information is known the remedies sought by this grievance are inappropriate and unjustified. The issue regarding former employees Burnette and Anderson are not relevant. Will be receiving undated information from the Area Office following a scheduled meeting regarding this contract proposal. Until that time any action would be based on emotion and hysteria as opposed to fact.

19. Management's Position
It is the responsibility of the Union to prove any contractual violations. The present situation is still being studied. Management maintains the right to determine the methods, means and personnel by which such operations are to be conducted.. consistent with applicable laws and regulations.... No present actions are in violation of the contract. However, the Unions express of concern is duly noted.

20. Union's Position
New equipment was scrapped to ensure that cost factors wuld favor contracting out activities. A test was done on the East Coast. The results of this test have not been shown because management is afraid cost analysis would not support acting out. Mangement has not standardized repair procedures since 1993. This was done intentionally. CRC has extended the life of containers reducing overall costs.

21. a. Management Official (Name and Title) Jacquelyn A. Cooper, Supervisor Maintenance CRC
21. b. Telephone Number (510) 251-3177
21. c. Signature

TransFORM PS Form 2608-A

The Postal Service holds mail in storage until the mail volume numbers are where they need them to justify the purchase of new processing equipment or modification of existing equipment. This mail was once held on the street and in the yard in vans or on the bulk belt systems. Now with the bar-code system they can just run the mail through the system until the necessary figures are reached. This maneuver is called economic value added.

The accounting system the Postal Service uses is fraudulent. The Whistle-blower Program is fraudulent.

What was happening in Oakland was happening on a much larger scale across the nation at these large P&DC's.

I am reporting to you what happened in Oakland. Multiply what I am telling you by ten or more and you will get some idea of what was happening in Chicago where the P&DC is ten stories tall or in New York, Detroit, D.C., or any other large P&DC across the country.

L.A. sent 2000 pieces of equipment to be repaired in Oakland at container repair. The equipment had sat so long outside that most of it had to be scrapped. It was recorded as being repaired. We scrapped it. This is the same way that the mail processing equipment is dealt with.

Were it not for the mail that was allowed to sit in the vans in the lot, on the street and in the bulk belt systems around the country, the mail volume figures would not be as high as they are. Once the machines were installed, the vans and the bulk belt systems disappeared. The mail is still there. Now they have a forever stamp that won't shock you when the price goes to $1.00 because they don't have to put the price on it.

The so called push for reform is a diversion, like Lance Armstrong. His rides were impressive to say the least, but he was just another diversion like the many expensive public relations gimmicks staged by the Postal Service. The Postal Service should be held accountable for the delivery of the mail...all of it. As it is the Postal Service is engaged in a partnership with big business and mass mail companies to defraud and disconnect the American public.

When I first started working at the Post Office as a custodian I worked the graveyard shift. We would punch in and go to the motel or across the street to the bar and shoot pool until break, then come in and work two hours, sleep for a hour, work two hours and then go home.

A manager got caught with his mouth full of pubic hair in the sack room. He and the lady he was with were promoted.

The Labor Relations manager was having a relationship with a woman who already had six kids. He had given her the keys to his office in the tower and was using the place like it was a motel. People were having sex on the elevators, in the janitor's closets in the air handlers. It was an animal-house!

The swing-rooms were just that ... Swing rooms. Cards and dominos would be played all night. If you were good you could make a little money. If you cheated you were dealt with in the parking lot

There were people living in the building. A supervisor almost had a heart attack when she opened a machine and found someone asleep inside. Another supervisor found someone asleep under her desk. One guy had hollowed out a space in the sack room, right in the middle; he had been camped out there for a year.

Chicago has ten stories. How many people did they have? People were allowed to relax, allowed to think that they could do at work what they did at home. This was done to divert attention from the corporate objective to control the mail. The people were and are expendable.

During the 60's and 70's African Americans and women were at the fore front. In the 80's and 90's Hispanics progressed up the ladder. Now it is the Asian along with a sprinkling of the Caribbean and Africans.

The 60's and 70's were the time of the civil rights movement and the free speech and student movements. The war in Viet Nam made things volatile to say the least. Ex- military people were working next to people with college deferments and anti-war protesters. It got dicey from time to time. Crisis management is the way things were run. When the "Big Bust", went down in Oakland most of the people busted for drugs were managers. One manager was picked up at the airport with a sack full of drugs

The people who came in during the late 80's and 90's missed the party, but they do have a clean work place. Now the system has been almost totally mechanized. The only way you could get your mail any faster would be for Scotty to beam it to you.

Now that the distribution has been automated, give the Post Office back to the people. If the corporations wish to pay for processing the mail, let them do that. The average man and the small mailer shouldn't be caught up in the in the wake, especially without a voice or representation.

"The modern U.S. Postal Service (LISPS) has its origins in the reorganization of the cabinet-level Post Office Department in 1971. It is governed by the USPS Board of Governors. The President appoints, and the Senate confirms, as many as nine governors to nine-year terms. No more than five Governors can belong to the same political party, so the board is officially bipartisan. These presidentially appointed Governors select a Postmaster General, who becomes a member of the Board. The Governor's then pick a deputy postmaster general, who also joins the Board. All told, there can be up to eleven Governors. The Board meets regularly, usually on a monthly basis, and there are also three standing committees that deal with more specialized issues. At this point in time, the Congress retains only minimal oversight of the Postal Service."

"The Postal Rate Commission (PRC) is the body that reviews the Postal Service's request for new postage rates, fees, and mail classifications. Interested parties (interveners) testify before the PRC on these matters. The PRC makes recommendations to the Board of Governors that are not easily disregarded or reversed. There are five commissioners appointed by the President and confirmed by the Senate for six year terms. A chairman is selected by the President. Like the board of Governors, the PRC is bipartisan: No more than three members can belong to one political party."

Again I must thank Mr. Shaw for his insight. This gives us insight into why the Postal bureaucrat views himself as omnipotent. The layers of officials shield each other from controversy and critical evaluation. All complaints are referred to the OIG who is the one who perpetrates and condones the actions of management in the absence of the Labor Relations Department. For an employee to get representation from the Merritt Systems Protection Board, the employee would first have to be terminated. How many Postal Workers can afford that?

People were railroaded at the end of their careers for the "good of the service." The employee who was nearly electrocuted was expected to go from repairing hampers and mail containers to being an electronic technician in the last three years of his career.

Many employees retired even though they could not afford to. It was either that or be fired for not passing or going for the training that was scheduled for them. The OIG condoned the actions of management on this issue.

Three of my friends died less that six months after being fired or forced to quit work. Until they made the decision to quit, these people were put under great stress. In maintenance that is dangerous.

During the years that the container repair center operated the Postal Service had no intention of profiting from the delivery of parcels. If the Postal Service had been profitable it would have kept UPS from issuing stock on the market. Postal Officials would not get in on the IPO. There are also a number of Postal officials who did quite well when FedEx made the agreement to work with the Postal Service.

Look at the graph that was provided courtesy of the Associated Press(next page).

January 7, 2006

Mailing

■ 39-cent first-class stamp reflects first hike since 2002

FROM STAFF AND WIRE REPORTS

Starting Sunday, your mail will be signed, sealed and delivered for mor than ever before.

The first rate increase since 2002 boost the cost of sending a first-class letter by 2 cents, to 39 cents. Postcar will go up 1 cent, to 24 cents.

The increase follows legislation passed in 2003 requiring the Postal Service to place $3.1 billion in an esc account this year. Congress will deter

Graph showing Postal Rate increases from the 60's until now.

During the years that the container repair center existed the Postal Service competed with FedEx and UPS for parcel delivery business, or so it seemed.

In actuality a criminal enterprise was in full flower. There were not uniform repair proceeders and container repair centers in different areas didn't communicate. Equipment was scrapped and reported as being repaired. New equipment was kept in storage while old equipment was kept in service. People got hurt and the safety program was a joke.

The acquisition of mail processing equipment, the planned obsolescence of the container repair centers, postal rate increases, the dismantling of the Labor Relations Department, conversion of the accounting system(twice), and the departure of Ms. Corcoran, and the Hatch Act have given birth to the "Forever Stamp".

The graph shows clearly the adjusted postal rates based on adjustments for inflation. During this time an enormous amount of mail processing equipment was purchased and scrapped. (I have included some photos of early 70's and 80's equipment at the end of the book).

The public and small mailers have been excluded from the process of determining rates. The relationships that the Postal Service has with the people who make the machines and the large mass mailing companies dictates that the Service's primary concern should be processing not delivery.

The Postal Service does not have enough carriers to deliver the amount of mail that they process. This is due to two things. The first is that much of the mail is still run through the system numerous times to increase the mail volume numbers. The second is if delivery was the priority and enough carriers were hired, the number of managers would have to be reduced because the mail processing machines have replaced the clerks. If the Postal Service were held accountable for delivery, the numbers would show that there are too many managers and other non-mail related jobs on the postal rolls.

Privatization is not the issue. Accountability is the issue. The Postal Service is not accountable to the people; it is accountable to the corporations. Ask Mr. Potter who he considers to be the primary customers of the Postal Service?

Putting things in perspective, I must admit that what was happening at the Post Office was easily overshadowed by the events that occurred at the end of the last century. However, the introduction of the "Forever Stamp" is a wake up call. It is an insult to the American public to tell them that they will be excluded "forever" from the process of determining rate increases.

Since the agreements between the corporations have been made, the Congress and the Senate, magazine mailers and little people like you and I, have been cut out. I say let them have it.

Let them have their deal, but let the little man mail for free! Or let the Carriers be the primary stockholders and make the Postal Service public. Contract out management. Hold the Postal Service accountable for delivery rather than allowing them to determine revenue based on how much mail they process. Make it a business rather than a slush fund for the Inspector General and the rest of the "Good Old Boy's Club".

Every postal rate increase that has been requested since the early 70's has been requested based on fraudulent data. The accounting system was changed in the 70's and then it was changed again in 98 to cover up a billion dollar loss. The system is based solely on the processing of the mail. Delivery is not important.

23% of the mail processed through the machines is not delivered. This does not include mail that is delivered to dead people, people who have changed address, businesses that no longer exist and mail that is sent to the "occupant". This mail is pre-paid and should not be processed through the machines anyway.

The American people and small mailers are being hoodwinked, bamboozled, fleeced and taken to the cleaners by a bunch of self-serving ingrates.

Allen Sanford

GOING POSTAL

DISCLOSURE OF INFORMATION
Page ii

INFORMATION ABOUT FILING A WHISTLEBLOWER DISCLOSURE
WITH THE OSC *(cont'd)*

- employees of the U.S. Postal Service and the Postal Rate Commission;
- members of the armed forces of the United States (i.e., non-civilian military employees);
- state employees operating under federal grants; and
- employees of federal contractors.

FIRST-HAND INFORMATION REQUIRED

In order to make a "substantial likelihood" finding (*see previous page*), OSC must be in possession of reliable, first-hand information. OSC cannot request an agency head to conduct an investigation based on an employee's (or applicant's) second-hand knowledge of agency wrongdoing. This includes information received from another person, such as when a fellow employee informs you that he/she witnessed some type of wrongdoing. (Anyone with first-hand knowledge of the allegations you want to report may file a disclosure in writing directly with OSC.) Similarly, speculation about the existence of misconduct does not provide OSC with a sufficient legal basis upon which to send a matter to the head of an agency. If you think that wrongdoing took place, but can provide nothing more than unsubstantiated assertions, OSC will not be able to go forward with the matter.

DE MINIMIS ALLEGATIONS

While an allegation might technically constitute a disclosure, OSC will not review or refer *de minimis* or trivial matters.

ANONYMOUS SOURCES

While OSC will protect the identity of persons who make disclosures, it will not consider anonymous disclosures. If a disclosure is filed by an anonymous source, the disclosure will be referred to the Office of Inspector General in the appropriate agency. OSC will take no further action.

MATTERS INVESTIGATED BY AN OFFICE OF INSPECTOR GENERAL

It is the general policy of OSC not to transmit allegations of wrongdoing to the head of the agency involved if the agency's Office of Inspector General has fully investigated, or is currently investigating, the same allegations.

COMPLETED DISCLOSURE FORMS CAN BE SENT TO OSC BY MAIL, AT: DISCLOSURE UNIT, OFFICE OF SPECIAL COUNSEL, 1730 M STREET, N.W. (SUITE 201), WASHINGTON, DC 20036-4505.

PLEASE KEEP A COPY OF DISCLOSURE MATERIALS PROVIDED TO OSC. *REPRODUCTION CHARGES UNDER THE FREEDOM OF INFORMATION ACT MAY APPLY TO REQUESTS PROCESSED BY OSC FOR COPYING OF COPIES OF MATERIALS IN OSC FILES.*

Substantial and specific danger to public safety (☐)

DISCLOSURE OF INFORMATION
Page 3

6. Please describe the agency wrongdoing that you are disclosing, indicating how the agency's actions fit within the type(s) of wrongdoing that you checked in item 5. *(Be as specific as possible about dates, locations and the identities and positions of all persons named. Also, please attach any documents that might support your disclosure. Continue on a separate sheet of paper if you need more space.)*

In October of 1989 I participated in the shutdown of the bulk belt system at the main mail facility in Oakland. I was president of the Maintenance Craft of the American Postal Worker's Union, Oakland Local.OSHA instructed that the system be removed as a result of the earthquake. Two parts of the system were eventually removed but maintenance on the system was suspended. The system was allowed to deteriorate to the point that mechanics had to use screwdrivers to turn the belts on. On October 10, 2002 an employee was nearly electrocuted while working on the equipment. The employee was a lower level employee and he was being forced to work on 430 volt live circuits without training and under threat of termination. When he was shocked he transmitted the accident over the hand held radio to the supervisor and the rest of us on the crew at the time. The employee attempted to file a CA-1 accident report but was discouraged from doing so by the supervisor who threatened to take diciplinary action if he did. In her response the manager, Portia Munn, stated that the accident was caused by the inadvertent actions of the employee. This was a lie. The system was unsafe and being used to store, hide, and delay the mail. This manager was submitting fraudulent data as if the equipment were fully operational. Vans full of mail have been found in the yard on numerous occasions. This is prepaid mail, advertising and magazines. People don't know it's comming, the Postal Service has been paid and the Postal Rate Commission does not hold them accountable for delivery. California was the seventh largest economy on the planet at the time the system was shut down. Oakland is a hub that transported all the mail in Northern California at the time. The maintenance department was submitting data as if the system was working properly. The mail was actually being run through the system repeatedly until the desired mail volume numbers could be compiled...FRAUD!!...Every Postal Rate encrease that has been requested sense 1989 has been requested based on fraudulent data. Postal Executives should take a pay cut and give the three billion dollars back.

DISCLOSURE OF INFORMATION
Page 4

PART 3: OTHER ACTIONS YOU ARE TAKING ON YOUR DISCLOSURE

Who are you? That is the question that I was asked by the guy in the Associated Press office in Berkeley. I had just explained to him that I thought that the postal rate increases were based on fraudulent data.

Who did I need to be? I began to ask myself, "Who do you need to be to become a "Whistle-blower". A "Whistle-blower", was the cause of Ms. Corcoran's departure. I suspect that in her case that she was set up because she was about to open Pandora's Box.

If I had walked in with my badge and said that I was from the F.B.I. this story would have been published *before* I left the office. I gave the F.B.I. the same evidence that I have presented in this complaint. I was told that I had done my homework well, but that no crime had been committed.

In addition to the F.B.I., I have submitted this matter to the Office of Special Council, the Senate, the Congress, E.E.O., the Postal Rate Commission and the original complaint went to the OIG's office.

A hostile environment was inherited by the OIG's office when it was created. Ms Corcoran was about to deal with the primary cause for the waste and corruption, "contracting". The way it is set up, the Postal Service will continue to buy new equipment in the name of mail processing, and charge more for equipment as long as they are able to charge more for stamps and other services. If the priority was delivery rather than processing, the purchase and modification of equipment would slow down drastically and provide a clear picture of how many people were needed to work at the post office, and what the real cost of delivering the mail is.

After Ms. Corcoran's departure the issue of waste fraud and mismanagement has been put on the back burner. "Whistle-blower", complaints are suppressed when they deal with management issues. A lot of the life-threatening equipment that maintenance personnel had to work on is now gone. Were it not for the efforts of these people and the chances they took, the Postal Service would not have the mail volume figures that they report today.

Complaint to OSHA. They were informed three days after the man was shocked. Haven't heard from then since. There are also two statements here from two managers in response to my E.E.O. complaint and a reply by the senior electronic technician. Read carefully.

U.S. Department of Labor   Occupational Safety and Health Administration
71 Stevenson Street, Suite 420
San Francisco, CA 94105
(800) 475-4020
Fax (415) 975-4331

Reply to the Attention of:

DATE: *10-9-2*

Allen Sanford,
1132 Ward Street
Berkeley, CA 94702

RE: USPS - Oakland P&DC/203583497

Dear Allen Sanford:

As the enclosed letter indicates, we have been advised by the establishment official that the hazards you reported to the Occupational Safety and Health Administration (OSHA) have been investigated and that corrective action has been taken.

With this information, OSHA feels the case can be closed on the grounds that the hazardous condition(s) no longer exist(s). If you do not agree that the condition(s) you reported have been satisfactorily corrected, please contact us within 10 calendar days. If we do not hear from you within that time period, we will assume that the condition(s) have been eliminated and we will close our case file.

Your action on behalf of safety and health in the workplace is appreciated.

Sincerely,

Leonard Limtiaco, Director
Enforcement & Investigations

Enclosure: Copy of the establishment's official response

EXHIBIT 8

SENIOR PLANT MANAGER
OAKLAND PROCESSING & DISTRIBUTION CENTER

UNITED STATES
POSTAL SERVICE

October 7, 2002

DAN MOONEY
OCCUPATIONAL SAFETY AND HEALTH ADMINISTRATION
71 STEVENSON STREET, SUITE 420
SAN FRANCISCO, CA. 94105

SUBJECT: Complaint No. 203583497

Dear Dan Mooney,

I am in receipt of your complaint letter, issuance date October 1, 2002, notifying us of an alleged hazard(s) as follow:

DESCRIPTION:

"Level 4 and Level 5 mechanics are directed to perform maintenance functions such as Box 42 mechanics, without proper safety training including training related to electrical safe practices and lockout tagout".

Response

Maintenance Mechanics levels 4 & 5, who are assigned to the bulk mail processing system, referred to as "Box 42", at the Oakland P&DC are expected to perform a variety of activities.

Upon entry into the maintenance craft, all maintenance mechanics (including levels 4 and 5) are required to complete a variety of safety related courses.

The Maintenance Department is committed to providing continuous safety training, to include LOTO and electrical safety, please see the attached policies on:

- Commitment to Safety
- Use of Personal Protective Equipment (PPE) & Lockout Tagout
- Electrical Safety
- Maintenance- Job Training

However, in this particular case, I discovered that management had made an oversight to ensure that all levels 4 and 5 mechanics were given the necessary LOTO training specific to the equipment to which they were required to work (Box 42). This has been corrected and documented. Please see attached training records for those individuals that were overlooked.

1675 7TH STREET RM 219
OAKLAND CA 94615-9997
(510) 874-8382
FAX: (510) 874-8644

EXHIBIT 9

- 2 -

I hope that this addresses your concerns and those of the complaint. In the event you need additional information, please do not hesitate to contact me at (510) 874-8282.

Sincerely,

Richard J. Blancas
(A) Senior Plant Manager

Attachments

cc: PSS
MM
MHR
MSHS
APWU

EXHIBIT 10

10/10/02

RE: USPS - Oakland P&DC/203593497

Dear Dan Mooney.

The response you recieved from Mr. Blancas is a lie.

This morning mechanic Copland was shocked on a motor starter.

Mr. Copland is a level 5 general mechanic. He was told by the supervisor that he need not fill out a CA-1 because he did not appear to be injured.

"Lock Out" "Tag Out" does not apply to box 42. It cannot be done. If "lock out" "tag out" were done the mail flow would stop. The intent of Box 42 is to keep the equipment moving.

As I said before there are no operational guidelines for box 42.

Right now Mr. Teeter, level 10 electronic technician is trieing to get everything to work right

EXHIBIT II

The best way to see what is going on is to come and let me show you.

You or your representative can get on a bike and we will ride a regular two 42 route so that you can see how big the lie you have been told is.

If Mr. Copeland had died this morning would that have been evidence enough?? 2

They have not sent you copies of the training records, or procedural guidelines. There are none!! Sincerely,

Allen J. Sanford

P.S. You should come unannounced or as a new employee.

Tell them to send you my record. Tell them to send you a copy of the training records for all level 4 mechanics. There are none!!

These people don't want you in the building because it is a mess!!

EXHIBIT 12

10/12/02

RE: USPS-Oakland P+DC
203583497

Dear Mr. Mooney...

No CA-1 was generated after Billy Copeland's accident. The Maintenance Craft Director, Mike Hines, was present when the supervisor admitted that Box 42 mechanics had not been trained. Mr. Hines was conducting an inquiry into why a CA-1 was not generated. Apparently the supervisor convenced Mr. Copeland, even in the presence of the union representative, not to submit a CA-1. This is a threat to the safety of everyone in maintenance. If managers are allowed to encourage people not to file CA-1 reports, what will happen when accidents like Mr. Copeland result in <u>death</u>?

EXHIBIT 13

For years mechanics have had to manually manipulate motor starters inside panels. This is how Mr. Copeland was shocked.

None of the level 5's currently doing the job has been trained in motor starters. The equipment has been neglected for a number of years. Only now, as this complaint is in process, is an effort being made to correct the problem.

There is only one man on the problem. This is "rediculous"!!

Where would we be if Mr. Copeland had died??

Sincerely,

Allen J. Sanford
General Mechanic,
Former Maintenance Craft Director
A.P.W.U.

EXHIBIT 14

I, ROYCE HARRIS, an African American male, am employed at the Oakland Processing & Distribution Center. My current position is Manager, Maintenance. I have been in this position for 2 years. My supervisory relationship to Mr. Allen Sanford during the time at issue in this complaint was as Maintenance Manager for all Plant Maintenance activities. As such, I was the third level manager to Mr. Sanford. I was aware that the complainant was an African American male. My knowledge of this matter is as follows: By way of this EEO I was made been aware of the fact that Mr. Sanford has expressed a desire to be detailed to a higher level for work performed while assigned to want is described as Box 42 assignment. Prior to this EEO, he has not expressed this desire (in writing nor verbal) to me, in person or through management channels. It is management's position that the skills required to perform the duties of the Box 42 assignment can range all the way from the PS-04 up to PS-09 maintenance level. The decision to use PS-05 maintenance mechanics to perform the core duties required for this assignment was made by me as Superintendent of Maintenance, over eight years ago. Based on the tasked required for the assignment, I viewed the assignment as an idea training ground for employees who wanted an opportunity to learn our bulk mail processing system and at the same time learn some valuable troubleshooting skills. Even though the bulk of the tasks required to perform this assignment simply involves clearing jams and re-starting conveyor systems by hitting reset buttons, if the assigned employees make good use of the time spent answering trouble calls, they can gain skills and knowledge needed for advancement.

In the event extensive electrical and/or electronic troubleshooting is needed To repair the Sack Sorters and Conveyor System, the Supervisor, Maintenance Operations has the responsible for ensuring that the appropriately trained personnel are assigned. Over the years, we have reserved the right to assign a wild range of employees to the Box 42, based on their demonstrated skill levels. This has included details from outside the maintenance department, as well as maintenance employees. In cases of detailed employees (maintenance or otherwise), all initial detail assignments they are started at the PS-05 level.

Page 1 of 2

7-3-04   AFFIDAVIT

I, Dennis Chin, Chinese American male, I am a Supervisor Maintenance Operations EAS-16 at the Oakland P & DC. I have been in this position for about 16 years.

The assignment for the maintenance mechanic on box 42 is to clear mail jams on the conveyors and to restart the conveyor belts and the sack sorter machine when the Sack Sorter Control can not restart the machines. The mechanics are assign different area to work daily according to their job skill level. When there is troubleshooting on electrical or electronics to be done the supervisor is notified and would assign a trained employee on the equipment to do the troubleshooting on the equipment.

I have no knowledge of any person being detail to higher level to work on box 42 since I was assign to this area of maintenance. It was coincidental at that time all the mechanics with this skill level were all black. When the Container Repair Center closed, the mechanics were reassigned to the Oakland Processing and Distribution Center. During the reassignment other race was assign to Box 42. Mr. Mario Castillo was detailed to level PS-05 from PS-03 pending promotion through the Merit Selection System upon passing of the required training such as Industrial Electrical Service (IES).

Mr. Summers and Mr. Pierce were promoted when the U.S. Postal Service had a Maintenance Work Force Realignment upgrading them from PS-06 to PS-07 and the PS-05 stayed at the same level. The other employees: Mr. Brown, Mr. Nolan, and Mr. Harris are all PS-05 employees.

I do not discriminate against anyone because of his or her race, age and gender. Everyone is assign to different task every day according to his or her training and job skill level.

This is a lie

8/30/01

AFFIDAVIT

To whom it may concern:

My name is Don Teeter. For the past 12 years I have been the Electronic Technician Level 9 (now 10), in charge of the Bulk Belt and Conveyor system (Box 42) of the Oakland P&DC on tour 2. I am one of only two ET's on all 3 tours who is qualified to do high level troubleshooting of the Programmable Logic Controllers, the communications software and bus, writing and diagnosing ladder logic issues and other sophisticated problems pertaining to Box 42. Before upgrading to Electronic Technician, I was a level 7 Mechanic assigned to the Bulk Belts and Conveyors, under the tutelage of Mat Brown, a long time mechanic assigned to Box 42. I am also trained and qualified to work on the Sack Sorting Machines (SSM), Tray Sorter (TSM), Automatic Facer Canceler Machine (AFCS), the Bar Code Sorter (BCS), the Flat Sorter 100 (FSM100), the Flat Sorter 1000 (FSM 1000), the Small Package And Bundle Sorter (SPBM), as well as many other specialized tasks including plant security, Telephony, Postal Service Television Network (PSTN), and Box 42 and Postal Police Closed Circuit Television Monitoring.

I became aware of the statement of our Manager of Maintenance, Royce Harris as to the requirements of proficiency to work on Box 42. I feel so strongly about this issue, that I volunteered to write this statement. I certify that was not approached by Mr Allan Sanford, or in any way coaxed to write this. But when I heard about the issue he is addressing, I felt compelled to add my input.

In my professional opinion, the Level 5 mechanics assigned to work on Box 42 are required to possess electrical/mechanical skills and understanding equal to and, in some cases, greater than Level 7 mechanics working on other machines. Although the job does include "clearing jams and re-starting conveyor systems by hitting reset buttons", it is very much more than that. The electromechanical systems requires that Box 42 mechanics are able to troubleshoot and repair relay faults, photosensor problems, clutch and clutch rectifier problems, ac power problems (up to 480 vac) and to make a determination whether problems are electromechanical in nature, or whether an electronic technician needs to be called to look at the control processing equipment. Without them, I, as the electronic tech, would not be able to keep the system, which is the heart of much of the mail coming into our facility, running.

The Bulk Belt and Conveyor System at the P&DC is an old tired system (actually obsolete, circa 1988) which is degrading rapidly. The mechanics are doing an admirable job at even keeping it running for the USPS.

EXHIBIT /8

In addition, and not a small point, the Bulk Belt and Conveyor System is an extremely complex system. Unlike other machines that Level 7 mechanics and Electronic Technicians work on, the learning curve is very long and steep. This is the reason that other Mechanics and Electronic Technicians cannot be assigned to this function. A mechanic must understand how the belts are supposed to work (under ideal conditions-which they never have been) let alone learning where all the belts are. It took me a full two years to learn the complexities of the operation-the sequential relationships, modes such as "through" and "store", "remote" and "local" operations, "head-end sensors" vs. "tail-end sensors", "high jam" vs. "junction control" indications. All this, in addition to the hard work of repairing 500 foot conveyor belts makes this one of the very most difficult jobs in the Maintenance Department.

Although I am white, virtually all of the mechanics assigned to the Bulk Belt and Conveyor System operation have been Black. They have not been accorded the pay grade deserving of them. Most of the mechanics on Box 42 are reaching retirement age. Some, including Mat Brown (who knows more about the system than the original designers) will soon be leaving. The Postal Service will be lost without them. The Postal Service is now demanding that these long-time employees, at great hardship to them, be tested and sent to school for jobs that they have been performing for years.

I cannot help but feel that the refusal to pay these employees level 7 pay (retroactively for the time they have served on Box 42), as well as the disrespect they are shown, is a crass and discriminatory attempt to save money at the expense of loyal and productive workers

Don Teeter
Electron Technician-10
USPS, Oakland P&DC, Tour 2

Sept 22, 2002

EXHIBIT 19

98

Let us look at what I am looking at. The earthquake, the man that was almost electrocuted, the accident being covered up by saying that the equipment was fully operational and that the man had been trained, failure to respond to Safety Hazard Reports, or grievances, and the use of the Hatch Act to avoid the issue by government officials.

The data provided by the award letter should have been enough to start an investigation. No investigation was conducted and diligent efforts were made to terminate my employment.

This is not a novel. This is a "Whistle-blower" complaint that is being submitted directly to the court of public opinion. It must be done this way because all avenues for complaint on the part of employees, consumers and small mailers has been and will be ignored.

At the end of this complaint I have submitted some of the documentation that I have accumulated while communicating with the Congress, the Senate, the Office of Special Council, O.S.H.A. the OIG's office, and grievance documentation that should show how managers were able to lie on paper after the Labor Relations Department was done away with.

Oakland is a small fish in a very large pond but Oakland is not an apparition. The same thing was going on in L.A. That is why they knew that they could send 2000 pieces of equipment to Oakland to be scrapped even though it was recorded as being repaired.

P&DC centers in the east are ten times larger than the one in Oakland and organized criminal activity has been institutionalized for a long time on the east coast. What happened in Oakland did not originate in Oakland. It took an earthquake and the stupidity of management to bring the truth to the light.

If the man had not been shocked, the E.E.O. complaint that I had filed in 2002 would have had no validity. Once the man was shocked and the attempt was made to intimidate him into not filing a complaint, the case was on.

Most recent reply from Senator Boxer and the Office of Special Cuncil.

BARBARA BOXER
CALIFORNIA

COMMITTEES:
COMMERCE, SCIENCE,
AND TRANSPORTATION

ENVIRONMENT
AND PUBLIC WORKS

FOREIGN RELATIONS

United States Senate

HART SENATE OFFICE BUILDING
SUITE 112
WASHINGTON, DC 20510-0505
(202) 224-3553
http://boxer.senate.gov/contact

September 28, 2007

Mr. A.J. Sanford
1132 Ward St
Berkeley, CA 94702-2250

Dear Mr. Sanford:

Thank you for contacting me about postal rate increases and the quality of federal postal service. I value your input and appreciate your efforts to bring this vital issue to my attention.

I share your concerns about postal costs and customer service problems. In response to letters like yours, I have worked to ensure that the United States Postal Service implements cost-cutting steps and service improvement programs.

Please know that I will keep your views in mind as I work with my colleagues in the Senate to ensure high quality postal service at affordable prices.

Thank you for taking the time to write to me. I look forward to hearing from you again in the future.

Sincerely,

Barbara Boxer

Barbara Boxer
United States Senator

BB:PLZ

1700 MONTGOMERY STREET	312 NORTH SPRING STREET	501 'I' STREET	2500 TULARE STREET	600 'B' STREET	201 NORTH 'E' STREET
SUITE 240	SUITE 1748	SUITE 7-600	SUITE 5290	SUITE 2240	SUITE 210
SAN FRANCISCO, CA 94111	LOS ANGELES, CA 90012	SACRAMENTO, CA 95814	FRESNO, CA 93721	SAN DIEGO, CA 92101	SAN BERNARDINO, CA 92401
(415) 403-0100	(213) 894-5000	(916) 448-2787	(559) 497-5109	(619) 239-3884	(909) 888-8525

PRINTED ON RECYCLED PAPER

U.S. OFFICE OF SPECIAL COUNSEL
1730 M Street, N.W., Suite 218
Washington, D.C. 20036-4505
202-254-3600

June 21, 2006

Mr. Allen J. Sanford
1132 Ward Street
Berkeley, CA 94702

  Re: <u>OSC File No. DI-06-2069</u>

Dear Mr. Sanford:

  The Office of Special Counsel has completed its review of the information you referred to the Disclosure Unit. You alleged violations of law, rule, or regulation, gross mismanagement, a gross waste of funds, and an abuse of authority by employees of the United States Postal Service, Oakland, California.

  The Special Counsel is authorized to receive disclosures from an employee, former employee, or applicant for employment of the federal government concerning a federal agency. 5 U.S.C. § 1213(a)(1). Employees of the United States Postal Service (USPS) are excluded from coverage of Title 5 by statute. Because you are an employee of the USPS, the Office of Special Counsel does not have jurisdiction.

  Should you wish to pursue this matter further, you may contact the United States Postal Service, Office of Inspector General, 1735 North Lynn Street, Arlington, Virginia, 22209-2020, (800) 654-8896.

  Accordingly, we are closing our file. Should you wish to discuss this matter, please contact me at (202) 254-3604.

        Sincerely,

        Catherine A. McMullen
        Chief, Disclosure Unit

CAM/cam

ABOUT THE AUTHOR

I was born in Berkeley, California in 1950. I graduated from Berkeley High School in 1968. I was student body vice-president.

I attended Merit College in Oakland, California and transferred to the University of California at Berkeley in the early 70's.

I majored in economics. I flunked out. I was constantly arguing with my professors about what they were teaching. At the time 10% unemployment was considered the norm. I did not agree because most of the unemployment at the time was due to discrimination, and not to the lack of skilled labor. When Bill Gates and Steve Jobs invented the lap-top I was proven to be correct. Unemployment is now 4%. In his speech Fed Chairman Ben Bernanky stated that the economics of the late 60's and early 70's was wrong. I feel vindicated.

Printed in the United States
By Bookmasters